DIRECTIVES
ON
FORMATION
IN
RELIGIOUS
INSTITUTES

**Congregation for Institutes
of Consecrated Life
and
Societies of Apostolic Life**

ST. PAUL BOOKS & MEDIA

Vatican Translation.

Printed and published in the U.S.A., by St. Paul Books & Media
50 St. Paul's Ave., Boston, MA 02130

St. Paul Books & Media is the publishing house of the Daughters
of St. Paul, an international congregation of women religious
serving the Church with the communications media.

2 3 4 5 6 7 8 9   98 97 96 95 94

Contents

Introduction

1. Religious Consecration and Formation

2. Aspects Common to All Stages of Religious Formation

3. The Stages of Religious Formation

4. Formation in Institutes Ordered Toward Contemplation: Especially Nuns (PC, n.7)

5. Questions Concerning Religious Formation

6. Religious Candidates to Priestly and Diaconal Ministry

INTRODUCTION

The Purpose of Religious Formation

1. The proper renewal of religious institutes depends chiefly on the formation of their members. Religious life brings together disciples of Christ who should be assisted in accepting "this gift of God which the Church has received from her Lord and which by his grace she always safeguards."[1] This is why the best forms of adaptation will only bear fruit if they are animated by a profound spiritual renewal. The formation of candidates, which has as its immediate end that of introducing them to religious life and making them aware of its specific character within the Church, will primarily aim at assisting men and women religious realize their unity of life in Christ through the Spirit by means of the harmonious fusion of its spiritual, apostolic, doctrinal and practical elements.[2]

A Constant Concern

2. Well before the Second Vatican Council, the Church was concerned about the formation of religious.[3] The council, in its turn, gave doctrinal principles and general norms in Chapter 6 of the dogmatic constitution *Lumen Gentium* and in the decree *Perfectae Caritatis*. Pope Paul VI, for his part, reminded religious that, whatever the variety of ways of life and of charisms, all the elements of a religious life should be directed toward the building up of "the inner man."[4] Our Holy Father John Paul II, from the beginning of his pontificate and in numerous discourses which he has given, has frequently taken up the matter of religious formation.[5] Finally, the Code of Canon Law has undertaken to indicate in more precise norms the exigencies required for a suitable renewal of formation.[6]

Postconciliar Activities of the Congregation

3. In 1969, the Congregation, in the instruction *Renovationis Causam,* expanded certain canonical dispositions then in force in order "to make a better adaptation of the entire formation cycle to the mentality of younger generations and modern living conditions, as also to the present demands of the apostolate while remaining faithful to the nature and the special aim of each institute."[7] Other documents published later by the dicastery even though they do not bear directly on religious formation still touch it under one or another aspect. These are *Mutual Relations* in 1978,[8] *Religious and Human Promotion* and *The Contemplative Dimension of Religious Life* in 1980[9] and *The Essential Elements of the Teaching of the Church on Religious Life* in 1983.[10] It will be useful to refer to these different documents, since the formation of religious must be given in complete harmony with the pastoral direc-

tions of the universal Church and of particular Churches and in order to assist in the integration of "interiority and activity" in the lives of men and women religious dedicated to the apostolate.[11] Activity "for the Lord" will thus not fail to lead them to the Lord, the "source of all activity."[12]

The Reason for this Document
and to Whom It Is Directed

4. The Congregation for Institutes of Consecrated Life and Societies of Apostolic Life deems it useful, and even necessary, to address this present document to major superiors of religious institutes and to their brothers and sisters charged with formation, including monks and nuns, all the more so since many of them have requested it. It does so in virtue of its mission of giving guidance to institutes. This can help them to elaborate their own programs of formation (*ratio*) as they are obliged to do by the general law of the Church.[13] On the other hand, men and women religious have the right to know the position of the Holy See on the present problems of formation and the solutions which it suggests for resolving them. The document has been enriched by numerous experiences since the Second Vatican Council, and it treats questions frequently raised by major superiors. It reminds all of certain requirements of the law with respect to present circumstances and needs. It hopes, finally, to be of special help to institutes which are coming into existence and to those which at this time have few means of formation and information at their disposal.

5. The document is concerned only with religious institutes. It deals with what is most specific in religious life, and it gives only one chapter to the requirements necessary for approaching the diaconate and priesthood. These have been

the object of exhaustive instructions on the part of the competent dicastery, which instructions are also pertinent to religious who are to be ordained for these ministries.[14] The document tries to give valuable directions for the religious life in its entirety. Each institute will have to make use of them according to its own proper character.

The contents of the document apply to both sexes except where it is obvious from the context and from the nature of things that it does not.[15]

1. RELIGIOUS CONSECRATION AND FORMATION

6. The primary end of formation is to permit candidates to the religious life and young professed first to discover and later to assimilate and deepen that in which religious identity consists. Only under these conditions will the person dedicated to God be inserted into the world as a significant, effective and faithful witness.[1] It is consequently proper to recall at the beginning of a document on formation what the grace of a consecrated religious life represents for the Church.

Religious and Consecrated Life
According to the Doctrine of the Church

7. "Religious life, as a consecration of the whole person, manifests in the Church a wonderful marriage brought about by God, a sign of the future age. Thus religious bring to perfection their full gift as a sacrifice offered to God by which

their whole existence becomes a continuous worship of God in love."

"Life consecrated by the profession of the evangelical counsels"—of which religious life is a species—"is a stable form of living by which faithful, following Christ more closely under the action of the Holy Spirit, are totally dedicated to God, who is loved most of all, so that having dedicated themselves to his honor, the upbuilding of the Church and the salvation of the world by a new and special title, they strive for the perfection of charity in service to the kingdom of God, and having become an outstanding sign in the Church, they may foretell the heavenly glory."[2]

"Christian faithful who profess the evangelical counsels of chastity, poverty and obedience by vows or other sacred bonds, according to the proper laws of institutes, freely assume this form of living in institutes of consecrated life canonically erected by competent Church authority, and through the charity to which these counsels lead they are joined to the Church and its mystery in a special way."[3]

A Divine Vocation for a Mission of Salvation

8. At the origin of the religious consecration there is a call of God for which there is no explanation apart from the love which he bears for the person whom he calls. This love is absolutely gratuitous, personal and unique. It embraces the person to the extent that one no longer pertains to oneself but to Christ.[4] It thus reflects the character of an alliance. The glance which Jesus turned toward the rich young man has this characteristic: "Looking on him, he loved him" (Mk 10:21). The gift of the Spirit signifies and expresses it. This gift invites the person whom God calls to follow Christ through the practice and profession of the evangelical counsels of chastity,

poverty and obedience. This is "a gift of God which the Church has received from her Lord and which by his grace she always safeguards."[5] And this is why "the final norm of the religious life" will be "the following of Christ as it is put before us in the Gospel."[6]

A Personal Response

9. The call of Christ, which is the expression of a redemptive love, "embraces the whole person, soul and body, whether man or woman, in that person's unique and unrepeatable personal 'I.'"[7] It "assumes, in the soul of the person called, the actual form of the profession of the evangelical counsels."[8] Under this form, those who are called by God give a response of love in their turn to Christ, their redeemer: a love which is given entirely and without reserve and which loses itself in the offering of the whole person as "a loving sacrifice, holy, pleasing unto God" (Rom 12:1). Only this love, which is of a nuptial character and engages all the affectivity of one's person, can motivate and support the privations and trials which one who wishes "to lose his life" necessarily encounters for Christ and for the Gospel (cf. Mk 8:35).[9] This personal response is an integrating part of the religious consecration.

Religious Profession: An Act of the Church Which Consecrates and Incorporates

10. According to the teaching of the Church, "by religious profession members assume by public vow the observance of the three evangelical counsels, are consecrated to God through the ministry of the Church and are incorporated into the institute with rights and duties defined by law."[10] In the act of religious profession, which is an act of the Church

through the authority of the one who receives the vows, the action of God and the response of the person are brought together.[11] This act incorporates one into an institute. The members there "live a life in common as brothers or sisters,"[12] and the institute assures them the help of a "stable and more solidly based way of Christian life. They receive well-proven teaching on seeking after perfection. They are bound together in brotherly communion in the army of Christ. Their Christian freedom is fortified by obedience. Thus they are enabled to live securely and to maintain faithfully the religious life to which they have pledged themselves. Rejoicing in spirit, they advance on the road of love."[13]

The fact that religious belong to an institute causes them to give to Christ and to the Church a public witness of separation with regard to "the spirit of the world" (1 Cor 2:12) and to the behavior which it involves, and at the same time of a presence to the world in keeping with the "wisdom of God" (1 Cor 2:7).

A Life According to the Evangelical Counsels

11. "Religious profession places in the heart of each one of you...the love of the Father: that love which is in the heart of Jesus Christ, the redeemer of the world. It is love which embraces the world and everything in it that comes from the Father, and which at the same time tends to overcome in the world everything that 'does not come from the Father.'"[14] "Such a love should fill each of you...from the very source of that particular consecration which—on the sacramental basis of holy baptism—is the beginning of your new life in Christ and in the Church: it is the beginning of the new creation."[15]

12. Faith, hope and charity enable religious, by means of their vows, to practice and profess the three evangelical coun-

sels and thus to give "outstanding and striking testimony that the world cannot be transformed and offered to God without the spirit of the Beatitudes."[16]

The counsels are, as it were, the main support of the religious life, since they express in a significant and complete way the evangelical radicalism which characterizes it. In effect, through the profession of the evangelical counsels made in the Church, the religious wishes "to be set free from hindrances that could hold him back from loving God ardently and worshiping him perfectly and...to consecrate himself in a more thoroughgoing way to the service of God."[17]

These touch the human person at the level of the three essential spheres of his existence and relationships: affectivity, possession and power. This anthropological uprooting explains why the spiritual tradition of the Church has frequently put them in relation with the three lusts spoken of by St. John.[18] The faithful exercise of them fosters the development of the person, spiritual freedom, purification of the heart, fervor of charity, and it helps a religious to cooperate in the construction of human society.[19]

The counsels lived in as authentic a manner as possible have a great significance for all people,[20] for each vow gives a specific response to the great temptations of our time. Through them, the Church continues to show the world the ways for its transfiguration into the kingdom of God.

It is therefore important that attentive care should be taken to initiate candidates for the religious life theoretically and practically into the concrete exigencies of the three vows.

Chastity

13. "The evangelical counsel of chastity assumed for the sake of the kingdom of heaven as a sign of the future world and a source of more abundant fruitfulness in an undivided

heart entails the obligation of perfect continence in celibacy.''[21] Its practice assumes that persons consecrated by the vows of religion place at the center of their affective life a "more immediate" relationship (*Evangelica Testificatio,* n. 13) with God through Christ, in the Spirit.

"The observance of perfect continence touches intimately the deeper inclinations of human nature. For this reason, candidates ought not to go forward nor should they be admitted to the profession of chastity except after really adequate testing and unless they are sufficiently mature, psychologically and affectively. Not only should they be warned against the dangers to chastity which they may encounter, they should be taught to see that the celibacy they have dedicated to God is beneficial to their whole personality.''[22]

An instinctive tendency of the human person leads to making an absolute out of human love. It is a tendency characterized by self-centeredness, which asserts itself through a domination over the person loved as if happiness could be secured from this possession. On the other hand, one finds it very difficult to understand and especially to realize that love can be lived in a total dedication of oneself, without necessarily requiring a sexual manifestation of it. Education for chastity will therefore aim at helping each one to control and to master his or her sexual impulses, while at the same time it will avoid a self-centeredness that is content with one's fidelity to purity. It is no accident that the ancient fathers gave priority to humility over chastity, since this latter can be accompanied, as experience has shown, by a hardness of heart.

Chastity frees the human heart in a remarkable manner (1 Cor 7:32-35), so that it burns with a love for God and for all people. One of the greatest contributions which religious can bring to humanity today is certainly that of revealing, by their life more than by their words, the possibility of a true dedication to and openness toward others, in sharing their joys, in being faithful and constant in love without a thought of domination or exclusiveness.

The pedagogy of consecrated chastity will consequently aim at:

—Preserving joy and thanksgiving for the personal love in which each one is held and is chosen by Christ.

—Encouraging frequent reception of the sacrament of Reconciliation, recourse to regular spiritual direction and the sharing of a truly sisterly or brotherly love within the community, which is brought about by frank and cordial relationships.

—Explaining the value of the body and its meaning, acquiring an elementary physical hygiene (sleep, exercise, relaxation, nourishment, etc.).

—Giving basic notions on masculine and feminine sexuality, with their physical, psychological and spiritual connotations.

—Helping in matters of self-control on the sexual and affective level but also with respect to other instinctive or acquired needs (sweets, tobacco, alcohol).

—Helping each one to profit by past personal experiences, whether positive, in order to give thanks for them, or negative, in order to be aware of one's weaknesses, in order to humble oneself peacefully before God and to remain vigilant for the future.

—Manifesting the fruitfulness of chastity, its spiritual fecundity (Gal. 4:19), which begets life for the Church.

—Creating a climate of confidence between religious and their instructors, who should be ready to listen to whatever they have to say and to hear them with affection in order to enlighten and encourage them.

—Helping them to act with prudence in the use of the communications media and in personal relationships which may present an obstacle to a consistent practice of the counsel of chastity (cf. Canons 277.2 and 666). It remains the responsibility not only of the religious to exercise this prudence, but also of their superiors.

Poverty

14. "The evangelical counsel of poverty in imitation of Christ who, although he was rich became poor for us, entails, besides a life which is poor in fact and in spirit, a life of labor lived in moderation and foreign to earthly riches, a dependence and a limitation in the use and disposition of goods according to the norm of the proper law of each institute."[23]

Sensibility to poverty is nothing new, either in the Church or in the religious life. What is perhaps new is a particular sensibility for the poor and for the poverty that exists in the world which characterizes religious life today. There exist today types of poverty on a large scale that are either experienced by individuals or endured by entire groups: hunger, ignorance, sickness, unemployment, the repression of basic liberties, economic and political dependence, corruption in the carrying out of offices, especially the fact that human society seems organized in a way which produces and reproduces these different kinds of poverties, etc.

In these conditions, religious are thrust into a closer proximity with respect to the most needy and impoverished, the same who were always preferred by Jesus and to whom he said that he had been sent[24] and with whom he identified.[25] This proximity leads them to adopt a personal and communitarian style of life more in keeping with their commitment to follow more closely the poor and humble Christ.

This "preferential option"[26] and evangelical choice of religious for the poor implies an interior detachment, a certain austerity in community living, a sharing at times in their life and struggles, without however forgetting that the specific mission of a religious is to bear "outstanding and striking testimony that the world cannot be transformed and offered to God without the spirit of the Beatitudes."[27]

God loves the whole human family and wishes to bring all together without exclusion.[28] For religious it is consequently a kind of poverty not to let themselves be bound within a certain milieu or social class. A study of the social teaching of the Church, and particularly that of the encyclical *Solicitudo Rei Socialis* and of the instruction *On Christian Liberty and Liberation*,[29] will be of assistance in making the required discernments for a practical actualization of evangelical poverty.

Education to evangelical poverty will be attentive to the following points:

—There are young people who before entering the religious life enjoyed a certain amount of financial independence and were accustomed to obtain by themselves all that they wished. Others find themselves at a higher level of life within a religious community than they had in their childhood or during their years of study or work. Instruction in poverty should take account of the history of each one. It should also be remembered that among certain cultures families expect to gain by what appears to them to be an advance for their children.

—It is of the nature of the virtue of poverty to be engaged in a life of work, in humble and concrete acts of renunciation, of divestiture, which render religious freer for their mission; to admire and respect creation and the material objects placed at their disposal; to depend upon the community for their level of life; to desire faithfully that "all should be in common" and "that to each one is given what is needed" (Acts 4:32, 35).

All this is done with the intent of centering one's life on the poor Jesus, who is contemplated, loved and followed. Without this, religious poverty, under the form of solidarity and sharing, easily becomes ideological and political. Only one who is poor of heart, who strives to follow the poor Christ, can be the source of an authentic solidarity and a true detachment.

Obedience

15. "The evangelical counsel of obedience, undertaken in a spirit of faith and love, in the following of Christ, who was obedient even unto death, requires a submission of the will to legitimate superiors, who stand in the place of God when they command according to the proper constitutions."[30] Further, all religious "are subject to the supreme authority of (the) Church in a special manner" and "are also bound to obey the supreme pontiff as their highest superior by reason of the sacred bond of obedience."[31] "Far from lowering the dignity of the human person, religious obedience leads it to maturity by extending the freedom of the sons of God."[32]

Religious obedience is at once an imitation of Christ and a participation in his mission. It is concerned with doing what Jesus did and at the same time with what he would do in the concrete situation in which a religious finds himself or herself today. Whether one has authority in an institute or not, one cannot either command or obey without reference to mission. When religious obey, they offer this obedience in continuity with the obedience of Jesus for the salvation of the world. This is why everything which in the exercise of authority or obedience indicates a compromise, a diplomatic solution, the consequence of pressure or any other kind of temporizing is opposed to the basic inspiration of religious obedience, which is to align oneself with the mission of Jesus and to carry it out in time, even if such an undertaking is difficult.

A superior who promotes dialogue, educates to a responsible and active obedience. All the same, it remains for the superiors to use "their own authority to decide and to prescribe what is to be done."[33]

For the teaching of obedience it should be remembered:

—That to give oneself in obedience it is first necessary to be conscious of one's existence. Candidates need to leave the anonymity of the technical world, to know themselves as they are and to be known as persons, to be esteemed and loved.

—That these same candidates need to find true liberty in order that they may personally pass from "what pleases them" to "what pleases the Father." For this, the structures of a formation community, while ever remaining sufficiently clear and solid, will leave ample room for responsible initiatives and decisions.

—That the will of God is expressed most often and pre-eminently through the mediation of the Church and its magisterium; and specifically for religious, through their own constitutions.

—That for obtaining obedience, the witness of the elder members in a community has greater influence on the young than any other theoretical consideration. Still, a person who makes the effort to obey as Christ did, and in Christ, can succeed in overcoming less edifying examples.

Education in religious obedience will therefore be given with all the clarity and exigency that is necessary so that one does not wander from the "way" which is Christ in mission.[34]

Religious Institutes: a Diversity of Gifts to Be Cultivated and Maintained

16. The variety of religious institutes resembles a "wide-spreading tree" which, beginning with a seed sown by God, "has grown up in the field of the Lord" and multiplied.[35] Through them the Church manifests Christ "to believers and unbelievers alike, Christ in contemplation on the mountain, or proclaiming the kingdom of God to the multitudes, or healing the sick and maimed and converting sinners to a good life or blessing children and doing good to all men, always in obedience to the will of the Father who sent him."[36]

The variety is explained by the diversity of the "charisms of their founders,"[37] which "appears as 'an experience of the Spirit,' transmitted to their disciples to be lived, safeguarded, deepened and constantly developed by them in harmony with the body of Christ continually in the process of growth. 'It is for this reason that the distinctive character of various religious institutes is preserved and fostered by the Church.'"[38]

There is thus no uniform way for observing the evangelical counsels, but each institute should define its own way, "keeping in mind its own character and purposes."[39] This is true not only with regard to the observance of the counsels, but with respect to all that concerns the style of life of its members in view of tending toward the perfection of their state.[40]

A Life Unified in the Holy Spirit

17. "Those who make profession of the evangelical counsels should seek and love above all else God, who has first loved us (cf. 1 Jn 4:10). In all circumstances they should take care to foster a life hidden with Christ in God (cf. Col 3:3), which is the source and stimulus of love of the neighbor, for

the salvation of the world and the building up of the Church.''[41] This love, which orders and vivifies the very practice of the evangelical counsels, is poured out in hearts through the Spirit of God, which is a Spirit of unity, of harmony and of reconciliation not only among persons, but also within the interior of each person.

This is why the personal life of a religious must not become dichotomized between the generic end of religious life and the specific end of the institute; between consecration to God and mission in the world; nor between religious life in itself on the one hand and apostolic activities on the other. There is no religious life existing concretely ''by itself'' upon which is grafted the specific end and the particular charism of each institute as subordinate additions. In institutes dedicated to the apostolate there is no pursuit of sanctity, profession of the evangelical counsels or life dedicated to God and to his service which is not intrinsically connected with the service of the Church and of the world.[42] Further ''apostolic and charitable activity is of the very nature of religious life'' to such an extent that ''the entire religious life...should be imbued with an apostolic spirit and all apostolic activity with a religious spirit.''[43] The service of one's neighbor neither divides nor separates a religious from God. If it is moved by a truly theological charity, this service obtains its value as service of God.[44]

And thus it can truly be said that ''the apostolate of all religious consists first in their witness of a consecrated life.''[45]

18. It will be the duty of each one to verify the way in which their activities in their own lives are derived from intimate union with God and, at the same time, confirm and strengthen this union.[46] From this point of view, obedience to the will of God, manifested here and now in the mission received, is the immediate means through which one can secure

for oneself a certain unity of life, patiently sought but never fully attained. This obedience is only explained by a resolve to follow Christ more closely, which is itself enlivened and stimulated by a personal love of Christ. This love is the interior principle of unity of all consecrated life.

The proof of a unity of life will be opportunely made in terms of the four great fidelities: fidelity to Christ and the Gospel; fidelity to the Church and to its mission in the world; fidelity to religious life and to the charism of one's own institute, and fidelity to humanity and to our times.[47]

2. ASPECTS COMMON TO ALL STAGES OF RELIGIOUS FORMATION

A. Agents and Environment of Formation

The Spirit of God

19. It is God himself who calls one to a consecrated life within the Church. It is God, who all through the course of a religious life, keeps the initiative: "He who has called you is faithful, and he will do it."[1] Just as Jesus was not content to call his disciples, but patiently educated them during his public life, so after his resurrection he continued through his Spirit "to lead them to the fullness of truth."[2]

The Spirit, whose action is of another order than the findings of psychology or visible history, but who also works through them, acts with great secrecy in the heart of each one of us so as later to be made manifest in fruits that are clearly visible: the Spirit is the truth who "teaches," "reminds" and "guides."[3] He is the Anointing giving desire, appreciation, judgment, choice.[4] The Spirit is the consoling advocate who "comes to assist us in our weakness," sustains us and gives us a filial spirit.[5] This discreet but decisive presence of the Spirit of God demands two fundamental attitudes: humility, which makes one resign oneself to the wisdom of God, and the knowledge and practice of spiritual discernment. It is, in fact, important to be able to recognize the presence of the Spirit in all the aspects of life and of history, and through human mediation. Among these last must be included openness to a spiritual guide; this openness is prompted by the desire of having a clear knowledge of oneself and by a readiness to let oneself be advised and directed with the intent of correctly discerning the will of God.

The Virgin Mary

20. The work of the Spirit has always been associated with the Virgin Mary, mother of God and mother of all the members of the People of God. It is through the Spirit that she conceived the Word of God in her womb; it was for the Spirit that she awaited with the apostles, persevering in prayer (cf. *Lumen Gentium*, nn. 52, 59) following the ascension of the Lord. This is why the presence of the Virgin Mary is encountered by religious from the beginning to the end of their formation.

"Among all persons consecrated unreservedly to God, she is the first. She—the virgin of Nazareth—is also the one most fully consecrated to God, consecrated in the most perfect way. Her spousal love reached its height in the divine motherhood through the power of the Holy Spirit. She, who as mother carries Christ in her arms, at the same time fulfills in the most perfect way his call: 'Follow me.' And she follows him—she, the mother—as her teacher of chastity, poverty and obedience.... If the entire Church finds in Mary her first model, all the more reason do you find her so—you as consecrated individuals and communities within the Church!'' Each religious is invited "to renew your religious consecration according to the model of the consecration of the very mother of God."[6]

A religious encounters Mary not only under the title of an exemplar, but also under that of a mother. "She is the mother of religious in being mother of him who was consecrated and sent, and in her *fiat* and *magnificat* religious life finds the totality of its surrender to and the thrill of its joy in the consecratory action of God."[7]

The Church and the "Sense of Church"

21. Between Mary and the Church there are many close bonds. She is its most eminent member, and she is its mother. She is its model in faith, charity and perfect union with Christ. She is a sign of sure hope and of consolation for the Church until the coming of the day of the Lord (cf. *Lumen Gentium*, nn. 53, 63, 68). Religious life is also associated with the mystery of the Church by a special bond. It pertains to its life and holiness.[8] It "is a special way of participating in the sacramental nature of the people of God."[9] One's complete gift to God "unites the religious 'to the Church and her mystery in a special way' and urges such a one to work with undivided dedication for the good of the entire body."[10] And the Church, through the mystery of its pastors, "besides giving legal sanction to the religious form of life and thus raising it to the dignity of a canonical state,...sets it forth liturgically also as a state of consecration to God."[11]

22. In the Church, religious receive that which nourishes their baptismal life and their religious consecration. In it, they receive the bread of life from the table of the word of God and

of the body of Christ. It was actually during the course of a liturgical celebration that St. Anthony, who is rightly deemed to be the father of the religious life, heard the living and efficacious word which led him to leave everything in order to undertake the following of Christ.[12] It is in the Church that the reading of the word of God, accompanied by prayer, establishes the dialogue between God and religious,[13] encouraging them to high aspirations and necessary renunciations. It is the Church which associates the offerings which religious make of their own life with the eucharistic sacrifice of Christ.[14] It is through the sacrament of Reconciliation celebrated frequently, finally, that they receive, from the mercy of God, pardon for their sins and are reconciled with the Church and their own community, which has been wounded by their sins.[15] The liturgy of the Church should thus be for them the summit to which an entire community is tending and the source from which flows its evangelical strength (cf. *Sacrosanctum Concilium,* nn. 2, 10).

23. This is why the task of formation is necessarily carried on in communion with the Church, of which religious are members, filially obedient to its pastors. The Church, "which is filled with the Trinity,"[16] as Origen says, is a universal communion in charity, according to its image and dependence on its source. It is from her that we receive the Gospel, which she helps us to understand, thanks to her tradition and to the authentic interpretation of the magisterium.[17] For the communion which is the Church is organic.[18] It remains, thanks to the apostles and to their successors, under the authority of Peter, the "lasting and visible source and foundation of the unity both of faith and of communion."[19]

24. It is therefore necessary to develop among religious "a manner of thinking" not only "with" but, as St. Ignatius of Loyola also says, "within," the Church.[20] This sense of the

Church consists in being aware that one belongs to a people on a journey:

A people which has its source in the Trinitarian communion, which is rooted in human history; which is based upon the foundation of the apostles and upon the pastoral ministry of their successors, and which recognizes in the successor of St. Peter the vicar of Christ and the visible head of the whole Church.

A people which finds in the Scriptures, tradition and the magisterium, the triple and unique channel through which the word of God comes to it; which longs for a visible unity with other Christian, non-Catholic communities.

A people which is not unaware of the changes that have occurred through the centuries or of the present legitimate diversities within the Church, but which seeks rather to discover the continuity and unity that are all the more real.

A people which identifies itself as the body of Christ and which does not separate the love for Christ from that which it should have for his Church, knowing that it represents a mystery, the very mystery of God in Jesus Christ through his Spirit poured out and communicated to humanity today and for all time.

A people which, as a consequence, does not accept being perceived or analyzed from a merely sociological or political point of view, since the most authentic part of its life escapes the attention of the wise men of this world.

And, finally, a missionary people, which is not satisfied with seeing the Church remain a "little flock," but is ever seeking to have the Gospel announced to every human being so that the world will know that "there is no other name under heaven given to us whereby we may be saved" (Acts 4:12), except that of Jesus Christ (cf. *Lumen Gentium*, n. 9).

25. A sense of Church also implies a feeling for ecclesial communion. In virtue of the affinity which exists between religious life and the mystery of a Church, "whose unity...in communion and service"[21] is assured by the Holy Spirit, religious, as "experts in communion," are "called to be an ecclesial community in the Church and in the world, witnesses and architects of the plan for communion which is the crowning point of human history in God's design."[22] This is brought about through the profession of the evangelical counsels, which frees the fervor of charity from every impediment and causes religious to become a prophetic sign of an intimate communion with God loved above all else; it is also effected through the daily experience of communion of life, prayer and apostolate, essential and distinctive constituents of their form of consecrated life, which makes them signs of fraternal communion.[23]

This is why, especially during the course of initial formation, "life in common, seen especially as an experience and witness of communion,"[24] will be deemed an indispensable milieu and a preeminent means of formation.

The Community

26. At the heart of the Church and in communion with the Virgin Mary, community life enjoys a privileged role in formation at every stage. Formation depends to a great extent on the quality of this community. This quality is the result of its general climate and the style of life of its members in conformity with the particular character and spirit of the institute. This means that a community will be what its members make it, that it has its own requirements and that before it can be used as a means of formation, it deserves to be lived and loved for what it is in the religious life, as the Church conceives it.

The basic inspiration is obviously the first Christian community, the fruit of the Pasch of the Lord.[25] But in tending toward this ideal, it is necessary to be aware of its requirements. A humble realism and one's faith should animate the efforts made during formation toward fraternal life. The community is established and endures not because its members find that they are happy together due to an affinity in thought, character or options, but because the Lord has brought them together and unites them by a common consecration and for a common mission within the Church. All adhere to the particular mediation exercised by the superior in an obedience of faith.[26] Moreover, it should not be forgotten that the paschal peace and joy of a community are always the fruit of death to self and the reception of the gift of the Spirit.[27]

27. A community is formative to the extent that it permits each one of its members to grow in fidelity to the Lord according to the charism of his or her institute. To accomplish this, the members must be clear among themselves on why the community exists and on its basic objectives. Their interpersonal relationships will be marked by simplicity and confidence, being based primarily upon faith and charity. Toward this end, the community is formed each day under the action of the Holy Spirit, allowing itself to be judged and converted by the word of God, purified by penance, constructed by the Eucharist and vivified by the celebration of the liturgical year. It strengthens its communion by generous mutual assistance and by a continuous exchange of material and spiritual goods in a spirit of poverty and with the help of friendship and dialogue. The community lives the spirit of its founder and the rule of the institute profoundly. Superiors will consider it their particular office to seek to build a community of brothers or sisters in Christ (cf. Canon 619). Then each one, aware of his

or her responsibility within the community, is moved to grow not only for self, but for the good of all.[28]

Religious in formation should be able to find a spiritual atmosphere, an austerity of life and an apostolic enthusiasm within their community which are conducive to their following Christ according to the radicalism of their consecration.

It is fitting to recall here the words of Pope John Paul II's message to the religious of Brazil: "It will therefore be good that the young, during the period of formation, reside in formative communities where there should be no lack of the conditions required for a complete formation: spiritual, intellectual, cultural, liturgical, communitarian and pastoral; conditions which are rarely found together in small communities. It is therefore always indispensable to keep drawing from the pedagogical experience of the Church all that can assist and enrich formation in a community suitable to the individuals and to their religious, and in some cases, priestly vocation" (*Insegnamenti*, IX, 2, pp. 243-44).

28. Here it is necessary to bring up the problem caused by inserting a religious formation community in a poor milieu. Small religious communities inserted in a working-class district on the periphery of certain large cities or in the inner city or in the more remote or poorer areas of the country can be a significant expression of "the preferential option for the poor," since it is not enough to work for the poor, but there is also the question of living with them and, as far as possible, like them. However, this demand should be modified at times according to the situation in which religious find themselves. First of all, it is necessary to insist as a general rule that the requirements of formation should prevail over certain apostolic advantages that come from an insertion into a poor milieu. It must be possible to realize and maintain solitude and silence, for example, which are indispensable during the

whole time of initial formation. On the other hand, the time of formation contains periods of apostolic activities where this dimension of religious life can find expression, on condition that these small inserted communities conform to certain criteria which assure their religious authenticity; that is, that they offer the possibility of living a truly religious life in accord with the ends of the institute; that, in these communities the life of communal and personal prayer and, consequently, times and places of silence can be maintained; that the motives for the presence of the religious be first of all evangelical; that these communities always be ready to respond to the needs of the superiors of the institute; that their apostolic activity not be primarily a response to a personal choice, but to a choice of the institute, in harmony with the pastoral work of the diocese, for which the bishop is primarily responsible.

It must be remembered, finally, that in countries and cultures where hospitality is held in particularly high esteem, a religious community, with regard to times and places, insofar as possible ought to be able to maintain its autonomy and independence with respect to its guests. This is undoubtedly more difficult to realize in religious houses of a modest dimension, but it should always be taken into consideration when a community makes plans for its communitarian life.

The Responsibility of Religious for Their Own Formation

29. It is the individual religious who holds the first responsibility for saying yes to the call which has been received and for accepting all the consequences of this response; this is not primarily in the order of the intellect, but of the whole of life. The call and the action of God, like his love, are always new; historical situations are never repeated.

The one who is called is therefore invited unceasingly to give an attentive, new and responsible reply. The journey of each religious will recall that of the people of God in Exodus and also that slow evolution of the disciples, who were "slow to believe"[29] but who, in the end, were burning with fervor when the risen Lord revealed himself to them.[30] This indicates the extent to which the formation of a religious should be personalized. It will therefore be a question of strongly appealing to the conscience and personal responsibility of each religious, so that they interiorize the values of religious life and at the same time the role of life which is proposed to them by the director of formation so that they find within themselves the justification for their practical choices and find in the Creator Spirit their fundamental dynamism. Therefore, a right balance must be found between the formation of the group and that of each person, between the respect for the time envisioned for each phase of formation and its adaptation to the rhythm of each individual.

Instructors or Formators (Superiors and Others Responsible for Formation)

30. The spirit of the risen Jesus is made present and active by means of a complex of ecclesial mediations. The whole of the religious tradition of the Church attests to the decisive character of the role of teachers for the success of the work of formation. Their role is to discern the authenticity of the call to the religious life in the initial phase of formation and to assist the religious toward a successful personal dialogue with God while they are discovering the ways in which God seems to wish them to advance. They should also accompany religious along the paths of the Lord[31] by means of direct and

regular dialogue, always respecting the proper role of the confessor and spiritual director in the strict sense of the words.

Further, one of the main tasks of those responsible for formation is to ascertain whether the novices and the young professed are being effectively followed by a spiritual director.

Formators should also offer religious solid nourishment, both doctrinal and practical, in keeping with each one's stage of formation. Finally, they should progressively examine and evaluate the progress that is being made by those in their charge, in light of the fruits of the Spirit. They must decide whether the individual called has the capacities which are required at this time by the Church and the institute.

31. In addition to a sound knowledge of Catholic faith and morals, "those who are responsible for formation need to have:

—"The human qualities of insight and responsiveness.

—"A certain experiential knowledge of God and prayer.

—"Wisdom resulting from attentive and prolonged listening to the word of God.

—"Love of the liturgy and understanding of its role in spiritual and ecclesial formation.

—"Necessary cultural competence.

—"Sufficient time and good will to attend to the candidates individually and not just as a group."[32]

Consequently, this office requires inner serenity, availability, patience, understanding and a true affection for those who have been confided to the pastoral responsibility of the instructor.

32. If there is a group of formators under the personal responsibility of the one who is in charge of formation, the individual members should act in harmony, keenly aware of their common responsibility. Under the direction of the supe-

rior, "they should cultivate the closest harmony of spirit and action," and should form with one another and with those in their charge, one united family.[33] No less necessary is the cohesion and continued collaboration among those responsible for the different stages of formation.

The work of formation as a whole is the fruit of the collaboration between those responsible for formation and their disciples. If it remains true that the disciple assumes a large part of the responsibility for his or her own formation, still this responsibility can only be exercised within a specific tradition, that of the institute, for which those responsible for formation are the witnesses and immediate exponents.

B. The Human and Christian
Dimension of Formation

33. In its Declaration on Christian Education, the Second Vatican Council set forth the aims and means for every true education in the service of the human family. It is important to keep these in mind in the reception and formation of candidates for religious life, since the first requirement for this formation is the ability to identify a human and Christian foundation with a particular person. Numerous failures in religious life can, in effect, be attributed to defects that were not perceived or overcome in this area. Not only should the existence of this human and Christian foundation be verified in one who is entering religious life, but it is necessary to assure that effective adjustments are made all during the period of formation, according to the evolution of the individuals and events.

34. The integral formation of a person has a physical, moral, intellectual and spiritual dimension. Its ends and exigencies are known. The Second Vatican Council gives an

account of them in the Pastoral Constitution *Gaudium et Spes*[34] and in the Declaration on Christian Education *Gravissimum Educationis.*[35] The Decree on the Formation of Priests *Optatam Totius* gives criteria that enable one to judge the level of human maturity required in candidates for the priestly ministry.[36] These criteria can be easily applied to candidates for religious life, considering its nature and the mission which a religious is called to fill within the Church. The Decree *Perfectae Caritatis*, on the appropriate renewal of religious life, recalls the baptismal roots of religious consecration;[37] and, from this fact, it implicitly allows for admission into the novitiate only those candidates who are already living all of their baptismal promises in a manner consistent with their age. Similarly, a good formation for religious life should confirm one's profession of faith and baptismal promises in all stages of life and particularly in its most difficult periods, when one is called to freely choose again what once was chosen forever.

35. Whatever the insistence placed upon the cultural and intellectual dimensions of formation by this document, the spiritual dimension retains its priority. "The principal purpose of formation at its various stages, initial and ongoing, is to immerse religious in the experience of God and to help them perfect it gradually in their lives."[38]

C. Asceticism

36. "Following in the footsteps of Christ leads to sharing ever more consciously and concretely in the mystery of his passion, of his death and of his resurrection. The paschal mystery should be, as it were, the heart of the programs of formation, insofar as it is a font of life and of maturity. It is on this foundation that the new person is formed, the religious

and the apostle.[39] This leads us to recall the indispensable need of asceticism in formation and in the religious life. In a world of eroticism, consumerism and all kinds of abuse of power, there is a need for witnesses of the paschal mystery of Christ, the first stage of which necessarily passes through the cross. This passage requires insertion of a daily, personal asceticism into an integral program of formation; this leads candidates, novices and professed to the exercise of the virtues of faith, hope, charity, prudence, justice, temperance and fortitude. Such a program is perennial and cannot go out of style. It is always contemporary and always necessary. One cannot live out one's baptism without adopting asceticism, much less be faithful to a religious vocation. This way will be pursued all the more actively if, as with the entire Christian life, it is motivated by a love of our Lord Jesus Christ and by the joy of serving him.

In addition to this, Christians have need of coaches who can assist them in running along the "royal way of the holy cross." They need witnesses who renounce what St. John has called "the world" and "its lusts," and also "this world," created and preserved by the love of its Creator, and some of its values. The kingdom of God, which is shown by religious life "to surpass all things that are here below,"[40] is not of this world. There is a need of witnesses to say so. During the course of formation this naturally assumes reflection upon the Christian meaning of asceticism and sound convictions about God and his relationship with the world that has come from his hands. This is because a blissful and naturalistic optimism must be avoided on the one hand and a pessimism oblivious to the mystery of Christ, creator and redeemer of the world, on the other.

37. Asceticism, moreover, which implies refusing to follow one's spontaneous and primary drives and instincts, is an

anthropological exigency before being specifically Christian. Psychologists have observed that the young especially have need of encountering opposition (instructors, regulations, etc.) in order to develop their personalities. But this is not simply true for the young, since the development of a person is never fully achieved. The pedagogy used in the formation of religious should help them to be enthusiastic for an enterprise that demands effort. It is in this way that God himself leads the human person whom he has created.

38. An asceticism inherent in the religious life, among other elements, calls for an initiation into silence and solitude; this is true also for institutes dedicated to the apostolate. They must faithfully comply "with the basic law of all spiritual life, which consists in arranging a proper balance of periods set aside for solitude with God and others devoted to various activities and to the human contacts which these involve."[41] Solitude, if it is freely assumed, leads to interior silence, and this invites material silence. The regulation of every religious community, not only of houses of formation, should absolutely provide for times and places of solitude and silence; these foster hearing and assimilating the word of God, and at the same time favor the spiritual maturation of the person and of a true fraternal communion with Christ.

D. Sexuality and Formation

39. Today's generations have often grown up in such integrated situations that boys and girls are not helped to know and appreciate their own respective wealth and limitations. Formation in this area is particularly important due to apostolic contacts of all kinds and the greater collaboration which has begun between religious men and religious women as well as present cultural currents. Early desegregation and close and

frequent cooperation do not necessarily guarantee maturity in the relationships between the two sexes. It will therefore be necessary to take means to promote this maturity and to strengthen it with a view toward formation for the observance of perfect chastity.

Moreover, men and women must become aware of their specific place in the plan of God, of the unique contribution which respectively they should make to the work of salvation. Future religious should thus be offered the possibility of reflecting on the role of sexuality in the divine plan of creation and salvation.

In this context reasons must be given and understood to explain why those who do not seem to be able to overcome their homosexual tendencies or who maintain that it is possible to adopt a third way, "living in an ambiguous state between celibacy and marriage,"[42] must be dismissed from the religious life.

40. God did not create an undifferentiated world. Creating the human person to his own image and likeness (Gn 2:26-27), as a reasonable and free creature capable of knowing and of loving him, God did not wish man to be alone, but in relation with another human person, woman (Gn 2:18). Between the two is established a "mutual relationship: man to woman and woman to man."[43] "The woman is another 'I' in a common humanity."[44] This is why "man and woman are called from the beginning not only to exist 'side by side' or 'together,' but they are also called to exist mutually 'one for the other.'"[45] One can easily see the importance of these anthropological principles, since there is a question of forming men and women who, through a special grace, have made a free profession of perfect chastity for the sake of the kingdom of heaven.

41. A "penetrating and accurate consideration of the anthropological foundation for masculinity and femininity" will aim at "clarifying woman's personal identity in relation to man, that is, a diversity yet mutual complementarity, not only as it concerns roles to be held and functions to be performed, but also, and more deeply, as it concerns her nature and meaning as a person."[46] The history of religious life bears witness to the fact that many women, within the cloister or in the world, have found there an ideal place for the service of God and others, conditions favorable to the expansion of their own femininity and, as a consequence, to a fuller understanding of their own identity. This growth in depth is to be pursued with the help of theological reflection and "the help that can come from different human sciences and cultures."[47]

Finally, for a clearer perception of the specific character of the feminine religious life, one should not forget that "the figure of Mary of Nazareth sheds light on womanhood as such by the very fact that God, in the sublime event of the incarnation of his Son, entrusted himself to the ministry, the free and active ministry of a woman. It can thus be said that women, by looking to Mary, find in her the secret of living their femininity with dignity and of achieving their own true advancement. In the light of Mary, the Church sees in the face of women the reflection of a beauty which mirrors the loftiest sentiments of which the human heart is capable: the self-offering totality of love; the strength that is capable of bearing the greatest sorrows; limitless fidelity and tireless devotion to work; the ability to combine penetrating intuition with words of support and encouragement."[48]

3. THE STAGES OF RELIGIOUS FORMATION

A. The Stage Before Entrance into the Novitiate

Rationale

42. In today's circumstances, generally speaking, it may be said that the analyses of *Renovationis Causam* remains valid: "Most of the difficulties encountered today in the formation of novices are usually due to the fact that when they were admitted they did not have the required maturity."[1] It certainly is not required that a candidate for the religious life be able to assume all of the obligations of the religious life immediately, but he or she should be found capable of doing so progressively. The possibility of making such a judgment justifies the time and means employed in reaching it. This is the purpose of the stage preparatory to the novitiate, no matter what name may be given to it: postulancy, pre-novitiate, etc. It pertains exclusively to the proper law of institutes to

determine the manner in which it is carried out, but whatever these may be, "no one can be admitted without suitable preparation."[2]

Content

43. Taking into account what will be said (nn. 86ff.) with respect to the condition of youth in the modern world, this preparatory stage, which can be prolonged without fear, should aim at verifying and clarifying certain points which will permit superiors to determine the advisability of and the time for the candidate's admission into the novitiate. Care should be taken not to hasten the time for this admission nor to defer it unduly, provided that it is possible to arrive at a certain judgment on whether the person is a promising candidate.

Admission is based upon conditions determined by the general law of the Church, though the institute's proper law can add others.[3] The requirements of the law are as follows:

—A sufficient degree of human and Christian maturity[4] for undertaking the novitiate without its being reduced to the level of a course of general formation based on a simple catechumenate. It can actually happen that some present themselves as candidates who have not completed their Christian initiation (sacramental, doctrinal and moral) and lack some of the elements of an ordinary Christian life.

—A general cultural foundation which should correspond to what is generally expected of young persons who have achieved the normal education of their country. It is particularly necessary that future novices attain a facility in the language used in the novitiate.

Since this is a matter of basic culture, it will be important to take into account the conditions of certain countries or social environments where the level of schooling is still relatively low, but where the Lord is nonetheless calling candidates to the religious life. Thus it will be necessary to promote the original culture carefully and not assimilate it into a foreign culture. It is within their own culture that candidates, whether male or female, must recognize the call of the Lord and respond to it in a personal way.

—A balanced affectivity, especially sexual balance, which presupposes the acceptance of the other, man or woman, respecting his or her own difference. Recourse to a psychological examination can be useful, taking into account the right of each individual to preserve his or her own privacy.[5]

—The ability to live in community under the authority of superiors in a particular institute. This capacity certainly will be verified further during the course of the novitiate, but the question should be posed in advance. Candidates should be well aware of the fact that other ways exist by which to give all of one's life to the Lord, apart from entering a religious institute.

Forms of Realization

44. These can be diverse: reception into a community of the institute without sharing all its life—with the exception of the novitiate community, which is not recommended for this except in the case of nuns; periods of contacts with the institute or with one of its representatives; common life in a house of reception for candidates, etc. However none of these forms should give the impression that those who are interested have already become members of the institute. In every way the persons accompanying the candidates are more important than the modalities of reception.

One or several religious endowed with the necessary qualifications will be designated by superiors to guide the candidates and to help them with the discernment of their vocation. These persons will actively collaborate with the directors of novices.

B. The Novitiate and First Profession

End

45. "The novitiate, by which life in the institute begins, is ordered to this, that the novices better recognize their divine vocation and one which is, moreover, proper to the institute, that they experience the institute's manner of living, that they be formed in mind and heart by its spirit and that their intention and suitability be tested."[6]

Taking into account the diversity of charisms and institutes, the end of the novitiate could be defined, in other words, as a time of integral initiation into the form of life which the Son of God embraced and which he proposes to us in the Gospel[7] under one or another aspect of his service or one or another of his mysteries.[8]

Content

46. "The novices are to be led to cultivate human and Christian virtues; they are to be introduced to a fuller way of perfection by prayer and self-denial; they are to be instructed to contemplate the mystery of salvation and to read and meditate on the Sacred Scriptures; they are to be prepared to cultivate the worship of God in the sacred liturgy; they are to be trained in a way of life consecrated by the evangelical counsels to God and humankind in Christ; they are to be educated about the character and spirit, purpose and discipline, history and life of their institute, and they are to be imbued with a love for the Church and its sacred pastors."[9]

47. As a consequence of this general law, the total initiation which characterizes the novitiate goes far beyond that of simple instruction. It is:

—An initiation into a profound and living knowledge of Christ and of his Father. This presupposes a meditative study of Scripture, the celebration of the liturgy according to the spirit and character of the institute, an initiation into personal prayer, so that its practice becomes habitual, and a relish for the great authors of the Church's spiritual tradition, without being limited to spiritual reading of a modern cast.

—An initiation into the paschal mystery of Christ through detachment from self, especially in the practice of the evangelical counsels according to the spirit of the institute, an evangelical asceticism joyfully undertaken and a courageous acceptance of the mystery of the cross.

—An initiation into a fraternal, evangelical life. It is, in effect, within a community that faith is deepened and becomes communion, and that charity finds its numerous manifestations in the concrete routine of daily life.

—An initiation into the history, particular mission and spirituality of the institute. Here, for institutes dedicated to the apostolate, there enters the fact that: "To complete the formation of the novices, in addition to the time mentioned in no. 1 (that is, the twelve months to be passed within the novitiate community itself), the constitutions can determine one or several periods of apostolic exercises to be spent outside the novitiate community."[10]

These periods have the purpose of teaching the novices to "realize in their lives in progressive stages that cohesive unity whereby contemplation and apostolic activity are closely linked together, a unity which is one of the most fundamental and primary values of these same societies."[11]

The arrangement of these periods should take into account the twelve months to be passed within the novitiate community itself, during which the novices "will not be occupied with studies and duties which do not directly serve this formation."[12]

The novitiate program of formation should be defined by the institute's proper law.[13]

It is not advisable that the novitiate be conducted within a milieu foreign to the culture and native language of the novices. Small novitiates are actually better, provided that they are rooted in this culture. The essential reason for this is to avoid a multiplication of problems during a period of formation in which the fundamental equilibrium of a person should be established and when the relationship between the novices and the director of novices should be comfortable, enabling them to speak to each other with all the nuances required at the outset of an intensive spiritual journey. Further, a transfer into another culture at this particular moment involves the risk of accepting false vocations and of not perceiving what may be false motivations.

Professional Work During the Course of the Novitiate

48. It is worth mentioning here the question of professional work during the course of the novitiate. In a number of industrialized countries, for motives which are at times justified by an apostolic intention and which may also be in keeping with the social legislation of these countries, candidates who are receiving a salary only ask their employer for a one-year leave of absence "for personal convenience" at the time of their entrance into the novitiate. This enables them to regain their employment if they should return to the world, and they do not, as a consequence, run the risk of becoming unemployed. At times this also leads to the reassumption of their

professional work during the second year of the novitiate under the guise of apostolic activities.

We believe that the following principle should be stated in this regard. In institutes which have two years of novitiate, the novices can exercise their profession full time only under the following conditions:

—That this work effectively corresponds to the apostolic finality of the institute.

—That it is assumed in the second year of the novitiate.

—That it corresponds to the exigencies of Canon 648.2, namely that it contributes to perfecting the formation of the novices for life in the institute and that it is truly an apostolic activity.

Some Conditions to Be Observed

49. The canonical conditions for licit and valid admission on the part of both the candidate and the competent authority must be rigorously observed. Conformity with these regulations can avoid many future difficulties.[14] With respect to candidates for the diaconate or priesthood, special care should be taken at this time so that no irregularity later affects the reception of Holy Orders—it being understood that major superiors of clerical institutes of pontifical right can dispense from irregularities not reserved to the Holy See.[15]

It should also be remembered that superiors must consult the proper ordinary and ask for testimony from him before admitting a secular cleric into the novitiate (Canons 644 and 645.2).

50. The circumstances of time and place necessary for the fulfillment of the novitiate are indicated by law. Its flexibility should also be kept in mind, always remembering, however, that prudence can advise what the law does not impose.[16]

Major superiors and those responsible for formation should know that current circumstances, now more than ever, require conditions of stability sufficient to enable the novices to grow and advance in spirit in a profound and peaceful way. This is all the more important because of the fact that many candidates have already had experience of life in the world. Novices actually have a need of being trained in the practice of prolonged prayer, of solitude and of silence. For all this, the element of time plays a determining role. They can have a greater need "to withdraw" from the world than "to go" to the world, and this need is not merely subjective. This is why the time and place of the novitiate will be organized so that the novices can find an atmosphere that is favorable to becoming deeply rooted in a life with Christ. But this is only achieved by becoming detached from oneself, from all that which opposes God in the world and even from those goods of the world "that undoubtedly deserve to be highly valued."[17] As a consequence, making the novitiate in an inserted community is completely discouraged. As we stated above (n. 28), the demands of formation must take precedence over certain apostolic advantages of insertion in a poor milieu.

Pedagogy

51. Not all the novices enter the novitiate at the same level of human and Christian culture. It will therefore be necessary to pay very close attention to each individual so that each advances at his or her own pace, and so that the content of formation and the way it is communicated are suitable to the one receiving it.

The Directors of Novices and Their Collaborators

52. The care of the novices is reserved solely to the director of novices under the authority of the major superiors.

He or she must be free from all other obligations that would impede the complete fulfillment of the role as educator. If he or she has collaborators, these depend upon the director in what concerns the program of formation and the conduct of the novitiate. Together with the director, they have an important role in discernment and decision.[18]

When secular priests or other religious from outside the novitiate and even laymen or laywomen are brought into the novitiate, either for teaching or for the sacrament of Reconciliation, they work in close collaboration with the director of novices, each keeping complete discretion.

The director of novices is the spiritual guide appointed for this purpose for each and all of the novices. The novitiate is the place of the director's ministry, and he or she should thus be permanently available to the novices. The director will be able to fulfill this task readily only if the novices are entirely free and open in his or her regard. Nevertheless, in clerical institutes neither the director nor his assistant may hear the sacramental confessions of the novices unless, in particular instances, they spontaneously ask him to do so.[19]

Finally, directors of novices should remember that psycho-pedagogical means by themselves cannot substitute for an authentic spiritual direction.

53. "Conscious of their own responsibility, the novices are to collaborate actively with their director so that they may faithfully respond to the grace of a divine vocation."[20] And, "members of the institute are to take care that on their part they cooperate in the work of training novices by the example of their life and by prayer."[21]

Religious Profession

54. During the course of a liturgical celebration, the Church, through the competent superiors, receives the vows

of those who make their profession and associates their offering with the Eucharistic Sacrifice.[22] The *Ordo Professionis*[23] gives the outline of this celebration, but it also leaves room for the legitimate traditions of the respective institutes. This liturgical action manifests the ecclesial roots of profession. Beginning from the mystery celebrated in this way, it will be possible to develop a more vital and profound appreciation of consecration.

55. During the novitiate, both the excellence and the possibility of a perpetual commitment in the service of the Lord will be brought out. "The quality of a person can be judged by the nature of his bonds. Consequently, one can joyfully say that your freedom is freely attached to God by a voluntary service, a loving servitude. And, as a consequence of this, your humanity attains its maturity. 'Extended humanity,' as I have written in the encyclical *Redemptor Hominis,* means the full use of the gift of freedom which we have received from the Creator when he called man, made to his own image and likeness, into existence. This gift finds its full realization in the unreserved donation of the human person, whole and entire, in a spirit of nuptial love toward Christ and, with Christ, toward all those to whom he sends men and women who are totally consecrated to him according to the evangelical counsels."[24] One does not give one's life to Christ on a "trial" basis. Moreover, it is he who takes the initiative in asking this of us. Religious bear witness to the fact that this is possible, thanks first of all to God's fidelity and to the fact that this renders them free and happy if their gift is renewed each day.

56. Perpetual profession presumes a prolonged preparation and a persevering apprenticeship. This justifies the Church's requirement that it be preceded by a period of temporary profession. "While still retaining its probationary

character by the fact that it is temporary, the profession of first vows makes the young religious share in the consecration proper to the religious state."[25] Consequently, this time of temporary profession has as its end the strengthening of the fidelity of the young professed, whatever may be the human satisfaction which they receive from their daily life "in the following of Christ."

The liturgical celebration should carefully distinguish the perpetual profession from the temporal profession, which should be celebrated "without any particular solemnity."[26] On the other hand, the perpetual profession is made "with the desired solemnity and in the presence of the religious and others,"[27] since "it is the sign of the indissoluble union of Christ with the Church, his spouse (cf. *Lumen Gentium,* n. 44)."[28]

57. All the legal dispositions with respect to the conditions for validity and for the time of temporary and perpetual profession must be observed.[29]

C. Formation of the Temporarily Professed

What Is Prescribed by the Church

58. With respect to the formation of those who are temporarily professed, the Church prescribes that "in individual institutes, after first profession the formation of all members is to be continued so that they may lead more fully the proper life of the institute and carry out its mission more suitably. Therefore, proper law must define the program of this formation and its duration, keeping in mind the needs of the Church and the circumstances of human persons and times to the extent this is required by the purpose and character of the institute."[30]

"The formation is to be systematic, adapted to the capacity of the members, spiritual and apostolic, doctrinal and at the same time practical, and when it seems opportune, leading to appropriate degrees both ecclesiastical and civil. During the time of this formation, duties and jobs which would impede the formation are not to be assigned to members."[31]

Significance and Requirements of this Stage

59. First profession inaugurates a new phase of formation, which benefits from the dynamism and stability derived from profession. For the religious, it is a matter of reaping the fruits of the preceding stages and of pursuing their own human and spiritual growth through the courageous execution of their responsibilities. Retaining the spiritual enthusiasm given by the preceding stage is all the more necessary, since in institutes dedicated to the apostolate the move to a more open lifestyle and to very demanding activities often runs the risk of disorientation and aridity. In institutes dedicated to contemplation, the risk is more apt to be a matter of routine, of weariness and of spiritual laziness. Jesus taught his disciples through the crises to which they were subjected. Through his repeated prophecies of his passion, he prepared them to become more authentic disciples.[32] The pedagogy of this stage will therefore aim at permitting young religious to make real progress by means of their experiences according to a unity of perspective and of life—that of their own vocation, at this time in their existence, with a view toward perpetual profession.

The Content and Means of Formation

60. The institute has the grave responsibility of providing for the organization and duration of this period of formation and of furnishing the young religious with favorable conditions

for a real increase in their donation to the Lord. In the first place, it will provide them a vigorous formational community and the presence of competent instructors. Actually, at this level of formation, in contrast to what was said regarding the novitiate (cf. n. 47), a larger community, well provided with means of formation and good guidance, is better than a small community without experts in formation. As in the whole course of religious life, religious must make efforts: to better understand the practical importance of community life in keeping with the vocation proper to their institute; to accept the reality of this life and to discover within it the conditions for their personal progress; to respect others in their differences; and to feel personal responsibility within this same community. Superiors will specifically designate one to be responsible for the formation of the temporarily professed, extending in a specific manner to this level the work of the director of novices. This formation should last for at least three years.

61. The following suggestions for programs are only indicative, and they do not hesitate to propose a high ideal considering the need there is for forming religious to meet the requirements and expectations of the contemporary world. It will be up to the institutes and to the formators to make the necessary adaptations to individuals, places and times.

In the program of studies, special attention should be given to biblical, dogmatic, spiritual and pastoral theology and in particular to deepening a doctrinal understanding of consecrated life and of the charism of the institute. The establishment of this program and its functioning should respect the internal unity of teaching and the harmonization of different disciplines. A religious should be aware of learning, not many sciences, but only one: the science of faith and of the Gospel. In this regard, a cumulative diversification of courses and disciplines should be avoided. Further, out of respect for individuals, religious should not be introduced prematurely into highly controversial questions if they have not as yet completed the courses needed to approach them peacefully.

The program will aim at suitably providing a basic philosophical formation that will permit religious to acquire a knowledge of God and a Christian vision of the world in close connection with the debated questions of our time. This will show the harmony which exists between the knowledge of reason and that of faith in the search for truth, which is one. In such conditions, religious will be protected from the ever threatening temptations of a critical rationalism on the one hand and of a pietism and fundamentalism on the other.

The program of theological studies should be judiciously conceived and its different parts should be well defined so that the "hierarchy" of the truths of Catholic doctrine is brought out, since they vary in their relationship with the foundations of the Christian faith.[33] The establishment of this program can draw inspiration from an adaptation of the suggestions made by the Congregation for Catholic Education on the formation of candidates for the priestly ministry,[34] taking care not to omit anything that could assist in the acquirement of a good knowledge of the faith and of a Christian life within the Church: history, liturgy, canon law, etc.

62. Finally, the maturation of a religious at this stage will require an apostolic commitment and a progressive participation in ecclesial and social experiences in keeping with the charism of their institute and taking into account the attitudes and aspirations of individuals. In the process of these experiences, religious should remember that they are not primarily pastoral ministers, but that they are in a period of initial formation rather than one that is more advanced and that their

commitment to an ecclesial and especially a social service is necessarily subject to the criteria of discernment (cf. n. 18).

63. Even though superiors are rightly described as "spiritual directors in relation to the evangelical purpose of their institute,"[35] religious should have a person available to them, who may be called a spiritual director or spiritual counselor, for the internal, even non-sacramental forum. "Following the tradition of the early fathers of the desert and of all the great religious founders in the matter of provision for spiritual guidance, religious institutes each have members who are particularly qualified and appointed to help their sisters and brothers in this matter. Their role varies according to the stage reached by the religious, but their main responsibilities are: discernment of God's action; the accompaniment of the religious in the ways of God; the nourishing of life with solid doctrine and the practice of prayer; and particularly in the first stage, the evaluation of the journey thus far made.[36]

This spiritual direction, which "cannot in any way be replaced by psychological methods"[37] and for which the council claims a "due liberty,"[38] should therefore be "fostered by the availability of competent and qualified persons."[39]

These provisions primarily intended for this stage in the formation of religious should continue for the rest of their lives. In religious communities, above all those which are large and especially where the temporarily professed are living, there must be at least one officially designated religious to assist their brothers and sisters with guidance of spiritual advice.

64. Some institutes have provisions for a more intense period of preparation prior to perpetual profession which includes a withdrawal from one's usual occupations. This practice merits encouragement and extension.

65. If, as is provided for in the law, young professed are sent to study by their superior,[40] "such studies should not be programmed with a view to achieving personal goals as if they were a means of wrongly understood self-fulfillment, but with a view to responding to the requirements of the apostolic commitments of the religious family itself, in harmony with the needs of the Church."[41] The course of these studies and the pursuit of degrees will be suitably harmonized with the rest of the program for this stage of formation, according to the judgment of major superiors and those responsible for formation.

D. The Ongoing Formation
of the Perpetually Professed

66. "Throughout their entire life religious are to continue carefully their own spiritual, doctrinal and practical formation, and superiors are to provide them with the resources and time to do this."[42] "Each religious institute therefore has the task of planning and realizing a program of permanent formation suitable for all its members. It should be a program which is not simply directed to the formation of the intellect, but also to that of the whole person, primarily in its spiritual mission, so that every religious can live his or her own consecration to God in all its fullness and in keeping with the specific mission which the Church has confided to them."[43]

Reasons for Ongoing Formation

67. Ongoing formation is motivated first of all by the initiative of God, who calls each one at every moment and in new circumstances. The charism of religious life in a determined institute is a living grace which must be received and lived in conditions which often are new. "The very charism

of the founders (*Evangelica Testificatio,* n. 11) appears as 'an experience of the Spirit,' transmitted to their disciples to be lived, safeguarded, deepened and constantly developed by them in harmony with the body of Christ continually in the process of growth.... The specific charismatic note of any institute demands, both of the founder and of his disciples, a continual examination regarding fidelity to the Lord; docility to his Spirit; intelligent attention to circumstances and an outlook cautiously directed to the signs of the times; the will to be part of the Church; the awareness of the subordination to the sacred hierarchy; boldness of initiatives; constancy in the giving of self; humility in bearing with adversities. Especially in our times that same charismatic genuineness, vivacious and ingenious in its inventiveness, is expected of religious as stood out so eminently in their founders.''[44] Permanent formation demands that one pay close attention to the signs of the Spirit in our times and that religious allow themselves to be sensitive to them in order to be able to respond to them appropriately.

Moreover, continued formation is a sociological factor which in our days affects all areas of professional activity. It very frequently determines whether one will remain in a profession or be obliged to take up another.

Whereas initial formation is ordered toward a person's acquisition of an autonomy sufficient for faithfully living a religious commitment, ongoing formation assists a religious in integrating creativity within fidelity. This is because a Christian and religious vocation demands a dynamic growth and fidelity in the concrete circumstances of existence. This in turn demands a spiritual formation which produces inner unity, but which is also flexible and attentive to the daily events in one's personal life and in the life of the world.

"To follow Christ" means that one is always on the road,

that one is on one's guard against sclerosis and ossification in order to be able to give a living and true witness to the kingdom of God in this world.

In other words, there are three basic motivations for permanent formation:

—The first arises from the very function of the religious life within the Church. There it plays a very significant charismatic and eschatological role that presumes on the part of religious men and women a special attention to the life of the Spirit, both in the personal history of each one and in the hopes and anxieties of others.

—The second comes from the challenges which arise from the future of the Christian faith in a world that is changing with increasing rapidity.[45]

—The third concerns the very life of religious institutes and especially their future, which depends in part upon the permanent formation of their members.

Its Content

68. Continued formation is a global process of renewal which extends to all aspects of the religious person and to the whole institute itself. It should be carried out taking into account the fact that its different aspects are inseparable from and mutually influential in the life of each religious and every community. The following aspects should be kept in mind:

—Life according to the Spirit, or spirituality: this must have primacy, since it includes a deepening of faith and of the meaning of religious profession. The annual spiritual exercises and other forms of spiritual renewal are thus to be given priority.

—Participation in the life of the Church according to the charism of the pastoral activities in collaboration with others involved in that activity locally.

—Doctrinal and professional updating, which includes a deepening of the biblical and theological perspectives of the religious, a study of documents of the universal and local magisterium, a better knowledge of the local cultures where one is living and working, new professional and technical training when appropriate.

—Fidelity to the charism of one's institute, through an ever-increasing knowledge of its founder, its history, its spirit, its mission and a correlative effort to live this charism personally and in community.

69. Sometimes a significant amount of permanent religious formation takes place in an interinstitutional context. In such cases it should be remembered that an institute cannot delegate to external organizations the whole task of continued formation for its members, since in many respects that formation is too closely tied to values proper to its own charism. Each institute, according to its needs and potentialities, should therefore create and organize various programs and structures for the formation of its own members.

Special Themes for Ongoing Formation

70. The following stages are to be understood in a very flexible manner. It will be useful to combine them concretely with those which may arise as a result of the unforeseeable initiatives of the Holy Spirit. The following are regarded as particularly significant stages:

—The passage from initial formation to the first experience of a more independent life, in which a religious must discover a new way of being faithful to God.

—The completion of about ten years of perpetual profession, when the risk of life becoming "a habit" occurs with the consequent loss of all enthusiasm. At this time it seems imperative that there be a prolonged period during which one withdraws from ordinary life in order to "reread" it in the light of the Gospel and the mind of one's founder. Various institutes offer their members such a period of intensifying their religious life in what is known as the "third year," "second novitiate," "second probation," etc. It is desirable that this time be passed within a community of the institute.

—Full maturity, which often involves the danger of the development of individualism, especially among those of an active and vigorous temperament.

—A time of severe crisis, which can occur at any age as a result of external factors (change of place of work, failure, incomprehension, feelings of alienation, etc.) or more directly personal factors (physical or psychic illness, spiritual aridity, strong temptations, crises of faith or feelings, or both at the same time, etc.). In such circumstances a religious should be helped so that he or she successfully overcomes the crisis in faith.

—A time of progressive withdrawal from activity when religious feel more profoundly within themselves the experience which Paul described in the context of moving toward the resurrection: "We are not discouraged; and even if, in us, the outward man is being corrupted, the inner man is being renewed day by day."[46] Peter himself, after he had received the immense task of feeding the flock of Christ, heard him say, "When you are old, you will stretch forth your hands, and another will gird you, and lead you where you would not wish to go."[47] Religious can live these moments as a unique opportunity for allowing themselves to be penetrated by the paschal experience of the Lord Jesus to the point of wishing to die "to be with Christ," in keeping with their initial choice: "that I may know Christ, the power of his resurrection and the fellowship of his sufferings, being made conformable to his death in order to come, if possible, to the resurrection from the dead."[48] Religious life follows no other way.

71. Superiors should designate someone as responsible for permanent formation in the institute. But it is also desirable that religious all during their lives have access to spiritual guides or counselors in accord with their course of initial formation and in ways adapted to their greater maturity and their actual circumstances.

4. FORMATION IN INSTITUTES ORDERED TOWARD CONTEMPLATION: ESPECIALLY NUNS (PC, n. 7)

72. What has been said in the preceding chapter is also applicable to the institutes which will be considered here, taking into account their particular charism, tradition and legislation.

The Place of These Institutes in the Church

73. "There are institutes which are entirely ordered toward contemplation in such wise that their members give themselves over to God alone in solitude and silence, in constant prayer and willing penance. These will always have an honored place in the Mystical Body of Christ, in which 'all members do not have the same function' (Rm 12:4), no matter how pressing may be the needs of the active ministry. For they offer to God an exceptional sacrifice of praise, they

lend luster to God's people with abundant fruits of holiness, they sway them by their example and they enlarge the Church by their hidden apostolic fruitfulness."[1]

In the midst of a particular Church, "their contemplative life...is their primary and fundamental apostolate, because it is their typical and characteristic way in God's special design to be Church, to live in the Church, to achieve communion with the Church and to carry out a mission in the Church."[2]

From the point of view of the formation of their members and for the reasons which have been given, these institutes deserve a very special attention with respect to both initial and ongoing formation.

The Importance of Formation in These Institutes

74. The study of the Word of God, of the tradition of the fathers, of the documents of the Church's magisterium and systematic theological reflection cannot be held in low esteem where individuals have chosen to direct their whole life toward the primary, if not exclusive, search for God. These religious, who are totally dedicated to contemplation, learn from Scripture that God does not cease to search for his creatures in order to become united with them and that in return the whole life of a person cannot be anything but an unceasing search for God. They patiently undertake this search. At the same time God renders his creatures able to become enamored with him despite the burden of their limitations and their gropings. There is consequently the task of helping these religious approach the mystery of God without neglecting the critical exigencies of the human mind. The certainties given by revelation on the mystery of God, the Father, Son and Holy Spirit, must also be brought out, while ever remaining humble before the quest that will never be completed until we shall

see God face to face for what he is. The main concern of these contemplatives is not and cannot be the acquisition of extensive knowledge nor the gaining of academic degrees. It is and must be that of strengthening their faith, "the substance of things to be hoped for, the evidence of things that are not seen."[3] In faith are to be found the roots and premises of an authentic contemplation. It is occupied with certainties on paths that are unknown: "Abraham left, not knowing where he was to go";[4] faith enables one to remain steadfast during the time of trial as if one saw him who is unseen.[5] Faith heals, deepens and expands the efforts of a mind which seeks and contemplates what now is only attained "through a mirror, in a dark manner."[6]

Some Points to Be Stressed

75. The program of formation in these institutes, after it has taken into account their specific character and the means suggested for remaining faithful to it, will insist upon certain elements as it gradually takes up the successive stages of formation. It should be noted from the outset that the course of formation among contemplatives will be less intensive and more informal because of the stability of their members and the absence of activities outside the monastery. It must also be noted that in the context of today's world one should expect in the members of these institutes a level of human and religious culture in keeping with the needs of our day.

Lectio Divina

76. More than their brothers and sisters dedicated to the apostolate, the members of institutes totally directed toward contemplation spend a good part of each day in a study of the Word of God and in *lectio divina,* under its four aspects of

reading, meditation, prayer and contemplation. Whatever may be the terms employed in the different spiritual traditions and the precise meaning that is given to them, each one of these steps preserves its uniqueness and necessity. *Lectio divina* is nourished by the Word of God, where it finds its point of departure and to which it returns. The seriousness of biblical study, for its part, guarantees the richness of the *lectio*. Whether this latter has for its object the text of the Bible itself, a liturgical text or a great spiritual page of Catholic tradition, there is a faithful echo of the Word of God, which must be heard and perhaps, in the manner of the ancients, even murmured. This initiation requires courageous practice during the times of formation and all the further stages depend upon it.

Liturgy

77. The liturgy, especially the celebration of the Eucharist and the Divine Office, has a privileged place in these institutes. If the ancients readily compared the monastic life with that of the angels, it was, among other reasons, because the angels are the "liturgists" of God.[7] The liturgy, where earth is united with heaven and which therefore provides a kind of foretaste of the celestial liturgy, is the summit to which the entire Church is tending and the font from which it receives all its strength. It does not take the place of all of the activity of the Church, but for those who "have time solely for the things of God," it is the place and privileged means for celebrating in the name of the Church, in adoration, joy and thanksgiving, the work of salvation wrought by Christ, a memory of which is periodically offered to us in the unfolding of the liturgical year.[8] Therefore, it should not only be carefully celebrated according to the rites and traditions proper to the different institutes, but it should also be studied

with regard to its history, the variety of its forms and its theological significance.

78. In the tradition of some of these institutes, religious receive the priestly ministry and celebrate the daily Eucharist even though they are not destined to exercise an apostolate. This practice finds its justification not only in that which concerns the priestly ministry, but also in that which pertains to the sacrament of the Eucharist.

On the one hand there is actually an inner harmony between a religious consecration and a consecration to the ministry, and it is legitimate that these religious should be ordained priests even if they do not exercise a ministry within or outside of the monastery. "The union in the same person of the religious consecration, which makes of one an offering to God, and the priestly character configures the individual in a special manner to Christ, who is at once both priest and victim."[9]

On the other hand, the Eucharist "is an act of Christ and the Church even if it is impossible for the faithful to be present."[10] And it consequently deserves to be celebrated as such, because "the reasons for offering the sacrifice are not to be understood solely in view of the faithful to whom it is necessary to administer the sacraments, but primarily in view of God, to whom a sacrifice is offered in the consecration of this sacrament."[11] Finally, it is necessary to retain the affinity that exists between a contemplative vocation and the mystery of the Eucharist. Actually, "among the works of the contemplative life, the most important consist in the celebration of the divine mysteries."[12]

Work

79. Work is a common law by which religious know they are bound, and it is fitting that during the period of formation

they develop an appreciation of this, since with respect to those with whom we are now concerned, formation is carried on within the interior of the monastery. Work in order to live is not an obstacle to the providence of God, who is concerned with the least details of our lives; rather it enters into his plans. It can be considered as a service to the community, a means of exercising a certain responsibility within it and of collaborating with others. It permits the development of a certain personal discipline and gives a kind of balance to the more interior activities that make up the daily routine. In systems of social analysis, which are becoming progressively more developed in different countries, work also allows religious to share in the national solidarity, from which no citizen has the right to withdraw. More commonly, it is an element of solidarity with all the workers of the world.

Work thus responds not only to an economic and social need, but also to an evangelical demand. No one in a community can identify his or her self with a percise work that risks becoming his or her own property. Instead, all should be ready for any work that can be asked of them.

During the time of initial formation, especially during the novitiate, the time reserved for work should not encroach upon that which is normally reserved for studies or other activities in direct connection with formation.

Asceticism

80. Asceticism has a special place in institutes exclusively dedicated to contemplation; religious in such institutes should be fully aware of the fact that, despite the exigencies of a withdrawal from the world which is proper to them, their religious consecration makes them present to humanity and to the world "in a deeper way...in the heart of Christ."[13] "The monk is he who is separated from all and united to all"[14]:

united with all because he is united with Christ; united with all because he hears in his heart the worship, thanksgiving, praise, anguish and sufferings of all humanity; united to all, because God calls him to a place where he reveals his secrets to humanity. Religious who are wholly dedicated to contemplation are thus not only present to the world, but also to the heart of the Church. The liturgy which they celebrate fulfills an essential function of the ecclesial community. The charity which animates them and which they strive to perfect at the same time quickens the whole Mystical Body of Christ. In this love they arrive at the first source of all that exists, the *amor fontalis;* and because of this they are at the heart of the world and of the Church. "Within the heart of the Church, my mother, I shall be love."[15] This is their vocation and their mission.

Measures to Be Taken

81. The general norm is that the whole cycle of formation, both initial and permanent, is carried on within the interior of the monastery. For these religious it is the most suitable place in which they can complete the path of conversion, of purification and of asceticism with the intent of conforming their life to Christ. This requirement also has the advantage of favoring the harmony of the community. It is, in effect, the whole community and not simply more initiated individuals or groups which should benefit from the advantages of a well-ordered formation.

82. When a monastery cannot provide this formation itself because of a lack of teachers or of a sufficient number of candidates, it will be useful to organize teaching programs (courses, meetings, etc.) in common with several other monasteries or convents of the same federation, of the same order or of a basically common vocation in one of these monaster-

ies or convents, according to a schedule that will be suitable to the contemplative nature of the monasteries concerned.

In every instance where the demands of formation conflict with the rule of enclosure, the current legislation should be maintained.[16] For the sake of formation, assistance can also be sought from externs to the monastery and even to the order, provided that they enter into the specific perspective of the religious whom they will instruct.

83. The association of convents of nuns with institutes of men, according to Canon 614, can also be of advantage in the formation of nuns. It guarantees fidelity to the charism, to the spirit and to the traditions of a common spiritual family.

84. Every monastery will take care to create conditions that are favorable to personal study and reading by providing the religious with a good library that is kept up to date and, in certain cases, through correspondence courses.

85. Orders and congregations of monks, federations of nuns, and monasteries and convents that are not federated or associated with others are requested to draw up a program (*ratio*) of formation which will be included in their own law and will contain concrete norms for its execution in keeping with Canons 650.1, 659-661.

5. QUESTIONS CONCERNING RELIGIOUS FORMATION

The following contains actual questions or positions, some of which are the result of a brief analyses and which, as a consequence, probably deserve to be further discussed, refined and expanded. The directions and principles of other matters are expressed here, but their concrete application can only be made on the level of particular Churches.

A. Young Candidates to Religious Life and Vocation Promotion

86. Young people are "the hope of the Church."[1] It has "so much to talk about with youth, and youth have so much to share with the Church."[2] Although there are adult candidates to the religious life, the majority of candidates today are between 18 and 25 years old. To the degree that they have been influenced by what is conveniently called "modernity," it seems that some of their common traits can be identified with sufficient accuracy. The portrait reflects a Northern and

Western model, but this model is tending to become universal in its strengths and weaknesses, and each culture will add touches to it that are required by its own uniqueness.

87. "The sensitivity of young people profoundly affects their perception of the values of justice, non-violence and peace. Their hearts are disposed to fellowship, friendship and solidarity. They are greatly moved by causes that relate to the quality of life and the conservation of nature."[3] Likewise, they have a thirst for freedom and authenticity. Generally, and at times ardently, they aspire toward a better world; there is no lack of those who are engaged in political, social, cultural and charitable associations in order to contribute to the betterment of humanity. If they have not been corrupted by totalitarian ideologies, they are for the most part keenly interested in the liberation of humanity from racism, underdevelopment, war and injustices. This attitude is not always—at times is far from being—motivated by religious, philosophical or political principles, but the sincerity of these youth and the depth of their generosity cannot be denied. Among youth may be found some who are marked by profound religious sentiment, but this sentiment itself needs to be evangelized. Finally, there are some, and these are not necessarily in the minority, who lead a sufficiently exemplary Christian life and are courageously engaged in the apostolate, already experiencing what it means to "follow Jesus Christ more closely."

88. Though this is so, their doctrinal and ethical frames of reference tend to be relative, and to such an extent that they do not always know very well if there are solid points of reference for attaining the truth about humanity, the world and things. The lack of the teaching of philosophy in schools is frequently a reason for this. Young people hesitate to say who they are and what they are called to become. If they have some

conviction about the existence of good and evil, the meaning of these words seems to be at odds with respect to what it was for preceding generations. There is frequently a gap between the level of their secular knowledge, which can be highly specialized at times, and that of their psychological growth and their Christian life. Not all have had a happy experience within their family considering the crises which have afflicted this institution, either where the culture has not been deeply influenced by Christianity, where the culture is of a post-Christian type where there is an urgent need of a new evangelization or even where the culture has long been evangelized. They learn much through images, and the present system of education encourages this at times, but they read less. It thus happens that their culture is characterized by a nearly total absence of a historical dimension, as if our world began today. They have not been spared by consumerism, with the deceptions which it begets. Succeeding, at times with difficulty, in finding their place in the world, some let themselves be seduced by violence, drugs and eroticism. It is becoming less and less rare to find young people among the candidates for religious life who have had unhappy experiences in this last domain.

89. One thus has an indication of the problems which the variety and complexity of this human background pose for vocation promotion and also for formation. It is the discernment of vocations that is the concern here. Above all, in certain countries, some candidates for the religious life present themselves because of a more or less conscious search for social gain and future security; others look upon the religious life as an ideal place for an ideological struggle for justice. Finally, there are others of a more conservative nature who look upon the religious life as if it were a place for saving their faith in a world which they regard as being

hostile and corrupt. These motives represent the reverse side of a number of values, but they need to be corrected and purified.

In the so-called developed countries, there is perhaps above all a need of promoting a human and spiritual balance based on renunciation, lasting fidelity, calm and enduring generosity, authentic joy and love. Here, then, is a demanding but necessary program for those religious who are charged with vocation promotion and with formation.

B. Religious Formation and Culture

90. The word *culture* in its general sense, according to the Pastoral Constitution *Gaudium et Spes,* can indicate "all those factors by which man refines and unfolds the manifold spiritual and physical qualities that enable him to master his condition and his destiny" (nn. 53-62).[4] This is why culture may be said to be "that by means of which the human person becomes more human," and that "it is always situated in an essential and necessary relationship with what the human person is."[5]

On the other hand, "while the profession of the evangelical counsels involves the renunciation of goods that undoubtedly deserve to be highly valued, it does not constitute an obstacle to the true development of the human person, but by its nature is supremely beneficial to that development."[6] There consequently exists an affinity between the religious life and culture.

91. Concretely, this affinity calls our attention to certain points. Jesus Christ and his Gospel transcend all cultures, even if they are entirely penetrated by the presence of the risen Christ and of his Spirit.[7] On the other hand, every culture should be evangelized, that is to say, purified and healed of the

wounds of sin. At the same time the wisdom which it contains has been surpassed, enriched and perfected by the wisdom of the Cross.[8] It will therefore be good in every region:

—To be attentive to the level of general culture of the candidates, without forgetting that one's culture is not limited to the intellectual dimension of a man or woman.

—To see how religious succeed in inculturating their own faith within the culture of their origins and to assist them to do so. This should not aim at transforming a house of formation for the religious life into a kind of laboratory of inculturation. Nevertheless, those responsible for formation cannot neglect being concerned with this in their guidance of those who have been entrusted to them. Since it is a question of personal education in their faith and of its taking root in the life of the whole person, they cannot forget that the Gospel frees the ultimate truth of the values contained in a culture and that the culture itself expresses the Gospel in an original manner and reveals new aspects of it.[9]

—To initiate religious who are living and working in a culture that is foreign to their own native culture into a knowledge and esteem for this culture in keeping with the recommendations of the Conciliar Decree *Ad Gentes*, n. 22.

—To promote within the young churches, in communion with all the members of the local church and under the guidance of its pastor, an inculturated religious life in keeping with the Decree *Ad Gentes,* n. 18.

C. Religious Life and Ecclesial Movements

92. "In Church communion the states of life by being ordered one to the other are thus bound together among themselves. They all share in a deeply basic meaning: that of being the manner of living out the commonly shared Chris-

tian dignity and the universal call to holiness in the perfection of love. They are different yet complementary, in the sense that each of them has a basic and unmistakable character which sets each apart, while at the same time each of them is seen in relation to the other and placed at each other's service."[10] This is confirmed by the many actual experiences of sharing not only of work, but also at times in prayer and at meals among religious and members of the laity. It is not our intent here to undertake a general study of this new development, but solely to consider the relations between religious and the laity under the aspect of ecclesial movements, due for the most part to the initiative of laymen and women.

Ecclesial movements, inspired by a desire to live the Gospel more intensively and to announce it to others, have always been manifest in the midst of the People of God. Some of these have been quite closely connected with religious institutes and share their specific spiritualities. In our day and particularly during recent decades, new movements have appeared that are more independent of the structures and style of the religious life than in the past; their beneficial influence on the Church was frequently recalled during the Synod of Bishops on the vocation and mission of the laity (1987), provided that they observe a certain number of criteria of ecclesiality.[11]

93. In order to retain a positive relationship between these movements and religious institutes, and all the more so because numerous religious vocations have come from these movements, it is important to reflect upon the following requirements and the concrete consequences which these involve for members of these institutes.

—An institute, as it was intended by its founder and as it has been approved by the Church, has an internal cohesiveness which it receives from its nature, its end, its spirit, its character and its traditions. This whole patrimony is the axis around which both the identity and unity of the institute itself[12] and the unity of life of each of its members are maintained. This is a gift of the Spirit to the Church which does not admit any interference or any admixture. A dialogue and sharing within the Church presumes that each institute is well aware of what it is.

—Candidates for the religious life who have come from one or other of these ecclesial movements place themselves freely under the authority of the superiors and formators legitimately commissioned for their formation when they enter the novitiate. Therefore they cannot simultaneously be dependent upon someone apart from the institute to which they now pertain, even though they belonged to this movement before their entrance. This is a matter of the unity of the religious institute and the unity of life of its novices.

—These exigencies remain after the religious profession, so as to avoid appearances of divided loyalties either on the level of the personal spiritual life of the religious or on the level of their mission. If these requirements are not respected, the necessary communion between religious and the laity risks degenerating into a confusion on the two levels mentioned above.

D. Episcopal Ministry and the Religious Life

94. This matter has taken on more current interest since the publication of the document *Mutuae Relationes* and the emphasis which John Paul II has, on several occasions, placed on the impact of the bishops' pastoral care for religious life.

The ministry of the bishop and that of a religious superior are not in competition. Certainly there exists an internal order of institutes which has its own sphere of competence for the upholding and growth of religious life. This internal order enjoys a true autonomy, but it is necessarily exercised within the framework of organic ecclesial communion.[13]

95. Actually, "there is acknowledged a rightful autonomy of life, especially of governance, by which they enjoy their own discipline in the Church and have the power to preserve their own patrimony intact.... It belongs to local ordinaries to safeguard and protect this autonomy."[14]

Within the context of this autonomy, "the proper law (of these institutes) must define the program of this formation and its duration, keeping in mind the needs of the Church and the circumstances of human persons and times to the extent this is required by the purpose and character of the institute."[15]

"Regarding the office of teaching, religious superiors have the competency and authority of spiritual director in relation to the evangelical purpose of their institute. In this context, therefore, they must carry on a veritable spiritual direction of the entire congregation and of its individual communities. They should accomplish this in sincere harmony with the authentic magisterium of the hierarchy."[16]

96. On the other hand, bishops, as "authentic teachers" and "witnesses of divine and Catholic truth,"[17] have a "responsibility for the doctrinal teaching of faith both in the centers where its study is promoted and in the use of means to transmit it."[18]

"It is the duty of bishops as authentic teachers and guides of perfection for all the members of the diocese (cf. *Christus Dominus,* nn. 12, 15, 35.2; *Lumen Gentium,* nn. 25, 45) to be the guardians likewise of fidelity to the religious vocation in the spirit of each institute,"[19] according to the norms of the law (cf. Canons 386, 387, 591, 593, 678).

97. The above is in no way opposed to the autonomy of life and particularly of government, recognized in religious

institutes. If, in the exercise of this jurisdiction, the bishop is limited by the respect which he must have for this autonomy, he is not on this account dispensed from watching over the progress that religious are making toward holiness. It is, in effect, the duty of a successor of the apostles, insofar as he is a minister of the Word of God, to call all Christians in general to the following of Christ, and especially those who have received the grace of following him "more closely" (Canon 573.1). The institute to which these latter belong already represents a school of perfection and a way toward holiness in itself and for the religious, but religious life belongs to the Church and, as such, pertains to the responsibility of the bishop. The relationship between a bishop and religious men and women, which is perceived generally at the level of the apostolate, is more deeply rooted in his office as a minister of the Gospel, a promoter of holiness within the Church and as a guardian of the integrity of the faith.

In this spirit and on the basis of these principles, it is fitting that the bishops of particular Churches should at least be informed by major superiors regarding current programs of formation in centers or regarding services for religious formation which are located within their pastoral territories. Every difficulty pertaining to episcopal responsibility or concerning the activities of these services or centers should be examined between bishops and major superiors, in keeping with the directives given in *Mutuae Relationes* (nn. 24-35) and in certain cases, with the help of the organs of coordination indicated in the same document (nn. 52-67).

E. Interinstitutional Collaboration

98. The first responsibility for the formation of religious belongs by law to each institute; it is the major superiors of

the institutes, with the help of qualified assistants, who must attend to this important mission. Each institute, moreover, should, according to the law, establish its own program (*ratio*) of formation.[20] Still, necessity has led some institutes on every continent to place their means of formation (personnel and institutions) in common in order to collaborate in such an important work, which they could no longer accomplish by themselves.

99. This collaboration is effected through permanent centers or periodic services. An interinstitutional center is a center of study for religious which has been placed under the collective responsibility of the major superiors of the institutes whose members participate in it. Its purpose is to assure the doctrinal and practical formation required by the specific mission of the respective institutes in accordance with their nature. It is distinct from the formation community proper to each institute and within which a novice and a religious are introduced into the communitarian, spiritual and pastoral life of the institute. When an institute participates in an interinstitutional center, a complementarity should exist between the formation community and the center so that an integral and harmonious formation is provided.

Centers of formation for a federation should observe the norms written in the statutes of the federation; however these are not the present concern. The same holds true for centers or study programs placed under the responsibility of a single institute, but which, as hosts, receive religious of other institutes.

100. Interinstitutional collaboration for the formation of young professed, for ongoing formation and for the formation of formators can be effected within the framework of a center. The formation of novices, on the other hand, can only be given under the form of periodic services, since the novitiate

community properly so-called must be a homogenous community proper to each institute.

Our dicastery intends to publish a special normative document later on dealing with the establishment of interinstitutional collaboration in the area of formation.

6. RELIGIOUS CANDIDATES TO PRIESTLY AND DIACONAL MINISTRY

101. The questions raised by this type of religious deserve to be examined separately because of their particular character. They are of three kinds. The first is regarding the formation of ministers as such; the second, the specific religious character of religious priests and deacons; the third, the insertion of the religious priest into the diocesan presbyterate.

Formation

102. In some institutes defined by their proper law as "clerical," it is proposed at times that the same formation be given to lay brothers and to candidates for the ordained ministries. On the level of the novitiate, a common formation for both even seems to be demanded at times by the specific charism of the institute. This has advantages both with respect to the quality and the completeness of the doctrinal formation

of the lay brothers and with their integration within the community. But in all such cases norms regarding the length and content of the preparatory studies for priestly ministry must be rigorously observed and followed.

103. "The formation of members who are preparing to receive holy orders is regulated by universal law and by the program of studies proper to the institute."[1] Religious candidates for the priestly ministry will thus comply with the norms of the *Ratio Fundamentalis Institutionis Sacerdotalis,*[2] and candidates for the permanent diaconate with the dispositions provided for this in the proper law of their institutes. The totality of this *ratio,* the major points of which are found in canon law,[3] will not be repeated here. It will be enough to recall some of the stages of the course of formation so that they may be observed by major superiors.

104. Philosophical and theological studies, whether taken successively or conjointly, should comprise at least six complete years so that two whole years are given to philosophical and four whole years to theological disciplines. Major superiors must be attentive to the observation of these norms, especially when they entrust their young religious to interinstitutional centers or to universities.

105. Even though the entire formation of candidates to the priesthood has a pastoral goal, they should have a pastoral formation, properly so called, which is adapted to the end of the institute. The program for this formation will be animated by the Decree *Optatam Totius* and, for religious called to work in cultures foreign to their own, by the Decree *Ad Gentes.*[4]

106. Religious priests dedicated to contemplation, whether monks or others, who are called by their superiors to serve their guests in the ministry of reconciliation or spiritual advice should be provided with a pastoral formation appropri-

ate to these ministries. They must also comply with the pastoral directives of the particular Church in which they live.

107. All the canonical conditions required of ordinands and all that pertains to them must be observed, taking into account the nature and obligations proper to the religious state.[5]

The Specific Religious Character
of Religious Priests and Deacons

108. "A religious priest involved in pastoral activity alongside diocesan priests should clearly show by his attitudes that he is a religious."[6] So that "what characterizes religious life and the religious and gives them a particular aspect"[7] may always be manifest in a religious priest or deacon, it seems that several conditions must be fulfilled; it will be useful for religious who are candidates for priestly and diaconal ministries to examine themselves on these during the time of their initial formation and in the course of their permanent formation:

—That they have a clear perception of and a firm conviction about the respective natures of the priestly and diaconal ministries, which pertain to the structure of the Church, and of religious life, which pertains to the sanctity and life of the Church;[8] at the same time there remains the principle that pastoral ministry is a part of the nature of their religious life.[9]

—That, for their spiritual life, they draw upon the sources of the institute of which they are a member and receive within themselves the gift which this institute is for the Church.

—That they bear witness to a personal spiritual experience which is inspired by the witness and teaching of their founder.

—That they lead a life in conformity with the rule of life which they have bound themselves to observe.

—That they live in community according to the law.

—That they are mobile and available for the service of the universal Church if the superiors of their institute call them to it.

If these conditions are respected, a religious priest or deacon will succeed in smoothly integrating these two dimensions of his unique vocation.

The Place of the Religious Priest Within the Diocesan Presbyterate

109. The formation of a religious priest should take into account his future insertion into the presbyterate of a particular Church, above all if he must exercise a ministry there, taking into account however, "the spirit of their own institute."[10] In effect, "the particular Church is the historical space in which a vocation is exercised in the concrete and realizes its apostolic commitment."[11] A religious priest can rightly deem it to be "the fatherland of his own vocation."[12]

The basic principles which govern this insertion have been given by the Conciliar Decree *Christus Dominus* (nn. 34-35). Religious priests are "cooperators with the episcopal order," and "in a certain sense [they] belong to the diocesan clergy inasmuch as they share in the care of souls and in the practice of apostolic works under the authority of the bishops."[13] Regarding this insertion, *Mutuae Relationes* (nn. 15-23) indicates the reciprocal influence between universal and particular values. Although religious are asked "even if they belong to an institute of pontifical right, to feel themselves truly a part of the 'diocesan family,'"[14] canon law recognizes the rightful autonomy[15] by which they maintain their universal and missionary character.[16]

Normally the position of a religious priest or of an institute to which the bishop has entrusted a mission or pastoral work within the particular Church must be regulated by a written agreement[17] between the diocesan bishop and the competent superior of the institute or the religious concerned. The same would hold for a religious deacon in the same situation.

CONCLUSION

110. This document has aimed at taking into account the experiments that have already been made since the council and, at the same time, at reflecting the questions that have been raised by major superiors. It reminds all of certain requirements of the law with respect to present needs and circumstances. In the end, it hopes to be of use to religious institutes so that all may advance in ecclesial communion under the guidance of the Pope and the bishops, to whom belongs "the ministry of discernment and harmony (cf. *Lumen Gentium,* n. 21) which involves an abundance of special gifts of the Holy Spirit and the distinctive charism of ordering the various roles in intimate docility of mind to the one and only vivifying Spirit."[1] In the first place it has been indicated that the formation of religious has for its primary end to initiate candidates into religious life and help them become aware of their identity as persons consecrated through their profession of the evangelical counsels of chastity, poverty and obedience in a religious institute. Among the agents of formation, primacy is given to the Holy Spirit because religious formation

in its origins and in its objectives is essentially a theological work. Insistence has been placed upon the need of forming qualified formators, without waiting till those who are presently in charge of this have completed their mandate. The primary role which the religious themselves and their communities play makes this task a privileged exercise of personal and communitarian responsibility. Several current questions have been raised. Though they have not all received a definitive response, they will at least provoke reflection. A special place has also been given to institutes which are wholly ordered toward contemplation because of their position at the heart of the Church and the special character of their vocation.

It now remains to ask for all, superiors, instructors, formators and religious, the grace of fidelity to their vocation, following the example and under the protection of the Virgin Mary. In its progress through the course of time, the Church "proceeds along the path already trodden by the Virgin Mary, who 'advanced in her pilgrimage of faith and loyally persevered in her union with her Son unto the cross.' "[2] The time of formation helps a religious to make this journey in the light of the mystery of Christ, which "shines in its fullness"[3] in the mystery of Mary, while at the same time the mystery of Mary "is for the Church like a seal upon the dogma of the Incarnation,"[4] as became clear at the Council of Ephesus. Mary is present at the birth and at the formation of a religious vocation. She is intimately involved in its whole process of growth in the Holy Spirit. The mission which she fulfilled in the service of Jesus, she fulfills for the benefit of his body, which is the Church, and in every Christian, especially those who strive to follow Jesus Christ "more closely."[5] This is why a Marian orientation, sustained by sound theology, will give the formation of religious the authenticity, the solidity and the joy without which their mission in the world cannot be fully accomplished.

In an audience granted to the undersigned Cardinal Prefect on November 10, 1989, the Holy Father approved the present document of the Congregation for Institutes of Consecrated Life and Societies of Apostolic Life and authorized its publication under the title "Directives on Formation in Religious Institutes."

Rome, Congregation for Institutes of Consecrated Life and Societies of Apostolic Life, Feast of the Presentation of our Lord, February 2, 1990.

Cardinal Jerome Hamer
Prefect

Archbishop Vincenzo Fagiolo
Secretary

Notes

Introduction

1. *Lumen Gentium,* n. 43.

2. Cf. *Perfectae Caritatis,* n. 18.3.

3. In chronological order: Congregation for Religious, Decree *Quo Efficacius,* Jan. 24, 1944; circular letter *Quantam Conferat,* June 10, 1944, n. 382; Apostolic Constitution *Sedes Sapientiae,* May 31, 1956, and the general statutes annexed to the constitution.

4. Paul VI, *Evangelica Testificatio,* n. 32; 2 Cor 4:16; Rm 7:22; Eph 4:24; *Enchiridion Vaticanum,* 996ff.

5. John Paul II in Porto Alegre, July 5, 1980; in Bergamo, April 26, 1981; in Manila, Feb. 17, 1981; to the Jesuits in Rome, Feb. 27, 1982; to the Capuchin masters of novices in Rome, Sept. 28, 1984; in Lima, Feb. 1, 1985; to the International Union of Superiors General in Rome, May 7, 1985; in Bombay, Feb. 10, 1986; to the International Union of Superiors General, May 22, 1986; to the Conference of Religious of Brazil, July 2, 1986.

6. Cf. Canons 641-661.

7. Congregation for Religious, Instruction *Renovationis Causam* (1969), Introduction.

8. Congregations for religious and for bishops, 1978.

9. Congregation for Religious.

10. *Ibid.*

11. *The Contemplative Dimension of Religious Life,* n. 4.

12. John Paul II to the Congregation for Religious and Secular Institutes, March 7, 1980.

13. Cf. Canon 659.2-3.

14. Congregation for Catholic Education, *Ratio Institutionis* (1970), nn. 1-2.

15. Cf. Canon 606.

Chapter 1

1. Cf. John Paul II to the International Union of Superiors General, May 7, 1985.

2. Canons 607, 573.1; cf. *Lumen Gentium*, n. 44 and *Perfectae Caritatis*, n. 1.5-6.

3. Canon 573.2.

4. Cf. 1 Cor 6:19.

5. *Lumen Gentium*, n. 43.

6. *Perfectae Caritatis*, n. 2a. On the divine vocation, see also *Lumen Gentium*, nn. 39, 43b, 44a, 47; *Perfectae Caritatis*, n. 1c; *Renovationis Causam*, Preface, n. 2d; Congregation for Divine Worship, Order of Religious Profession, nn. I, 57, 62, 67, 85, 140, 142; II, 65, 72; Appendix; *ibid.*, Order for the Consecration of a Virgin, nn. 17, 20; *Evangelica Testificatio*, nn. 3, 6, 8, 12, 19, 31, 55; congregations for religious and for bishops, *Directives for the Mutual Relations Between Bishops and Religious in the Church*, n. 8f; Canons 574.2, 575; Congregation for Religious, *Essential Elements in the Church's Teaching on Religious Life as Applied to Institutes Dedicated to Works of the Apostolate* (1983), nn. 2, 5, 6, 7, 12, 14, 23, 44, 53; John Paul II, Apostolic Exhortation *Redemptionis Donum* (1984), nn. 3c, 6b, 7d, 10c, 16a.

7. *Redemptionis Donum*, n. 3.

8. *Ibid.*, n. 8.

9. On the personal response, see also *Lumen Gentium*, nn. 44a, 46b, 47; *Perfectae Caritatis*, n. 1c; *Renovationis Causam*, nn. 2a, c, 13.1; *Order of Religious Profession*, nn. 1, 7, 80; *Evangelica Testificatio*, nn. 1, 4, 7, 8, 31; Canon 573.1; *Essential Elements*, nn. 4, 5, 30, 44; 44-9; *Redemptionis Donum*, nn. 7a, 8b, 9b.

10. Canon 654.

11. Cf. *Essential Elements*, nn. 13-17.

12. Canon 607.2.

13. *Lumen Gentium*, n. 43a. On the ministry of the Church in the religious consecration, see also *Lumen Gentium*, nn. 44a, 45c; *Perfectae Caritatis*, nn. 1bc; 5b, 11a; Order of Religious Profession, Appendix; Mass on Day of Perpetual Profession, n. 1; *Rite of Profession*, n. 5; Order for the Consecration of a Virgin, n. 16; *Evangelica Testificatio*, nn. 7, 47; *Mutual Relations*, n. 8a; Canons 573.2, 576, 598, 600-602; *Essential Elements*, nn. 7, 8, 11, 13, 40, 42; *Redemptionis Donum*, n. 7ab, 14c.

14. *Redemptionis Donum*, n. 9.

15. *Ibid.*, n. 8.

16. *Lumen Gentium*, n. 31.

17. *Ibid.*, n. 44.

18. Cf. 1 Jn 2:15-17.

19. Cf. *Lumen Gentium*, n. 46.

20. Cf. *ibid.*, nn. 39, 42, 43.

21. Canon 599.

22. *Perfectae Caritatis*, n. 12.

23. Canon 600.

24. Cf. Lk 4:6-21.

25. Cf. *ibid.*, 7:18-23.

26. Puebla Documents, 733-735.

27. John Paul II, *Solicitudo Rei Socialis*, n. 41; see also *Lumen Gentium*, n. 31.

28. Cf. *Gaudium et Spes*, n. 32.

29. Congregation for the Doctrine of the Faith, March 22, 1986.

30. Canon 601.

31. Canon 590.1-2.

32. *Perfectae Caritatis*, n. 14.

33. *Ibid.*, n. 14.

34. Cf. Jn 14:16.

35. *Lumen Gentium*, n. 43.

36. *Ibid.*, n. 46.

37. *Evangelica Testificatio,* n. 11; cf. Introduction, note 4, above.

38. *Mutual Relations*, n. 11; cf. Introduction, note 8, above.

39. Canon 598.1.

40. Cf. Canon 598.2.

41. *Perfectae Caritatis*, n. 6.

42. Cf. *ibid.*, n. 5.

43. *Ibid.*, n. 8.

44. St. Thomas, *Summa Theologica* IIa, IIae, Q. 188; a. 1 and 2.

45. Canon 673.

46. Cf. *Perfectae Caritatis*, n. 8.

47. Cf. Congregation for Religious, "Religious and Human Promotion" (1980), nn. 13-21; cf. Introduction, note 9, above.

Chapter 2

1. 1 Thes 5:23-24; 2 Thes 3:3.

2. Jn 16:13.

3. Cf. Jn 14:26, 16:12.

4. Cf. 1 Jn 2:20-27.

5. Cf. Rm 8:15-26.

6. *Redemptionis Donum*, n. 17.

7. *Essential Elements*, II, n. 53; cf. Introduction, note 10, above; *Lumen Gentium*, n. 53 and Canon 663.4.

8. Cf. *Lumen Gentium*, n. 44.

9. *Mutual Relations*, n. 10; cf. Introduction, note 8.

10. *Ibid.;* cf. *Lumen Gentium*, n. 44 and Canon 678.

11. *Lumen Gentium*, n. 45; cf. *Mutual Relations*, n. 8 and Introduction, note 8, above.

12. Cf. St. Athanasius, *Life of St. Anthony, Patrologia Graeca*, 26: 841-845.

13. Cf. *Dei Verbum*, n. 25.

14. Cf. *Lumen Gentium*, n. 45.

15. Cf. *Lumen Gentium*, n. 11.

16. *Patrologia Graeca*, 12:1265.

17. Cf. *Dei Verbum*, n. 10.

18. Cf. *Mutual Relations,* n. 5; cf. Introduction, note 8, above.

19. *Lumen Gentium*, n. 18.

20. Spiritual Exercises, 351-352.

21. *Lumen Gentium*, n. 4.

22. *Religious and Human Promotion*, n. 24; cf. Introduction, note 9, above.

23. *Ibid.*, cf. also Puebla Documents, 211-219.

24. *Religious and Human Promotion*, n. 33c; cf. Introduction, note 9, above; also Canon 602.

25. Cf. Acts 2:42; *Perfectae Caritatis*, n. 15; Canon 602ff.; *Essential Elements*, nn. 18-22.

26. Cf. Canons 601, 618-619; *Perfectae Caritatis*, n. 14.

27. Cf. Jn 12:24; Gal 5:22.

28. *Evangelica Testificatio*, nn. 32-34; cf. Introduction, note 4, above; *Essential Elements*, nn. 18-22.

29. Lk 24:25.

30. Cf. Lk 24:32.

31. Cf. Tb 5:10, 17, 22.

32. *The Contemplative Dimension*, n. 20; cf. Introduction, note 9, above.

33. *Optatam Totius,* n. 5b.

34. Cf. *Gaudium et Spes*, nn. 12-22, 61.

35. Cf. *Gravissimum Educationis*, nn. 1-2.

36. Cf. *Optatam Totius*, n. 11.

37. Cf. *Perfectae Caritatis*, n. 5.

38. *The Contemplative Dimension*, n. 17; cf. Introduction, note 9, above.

39. John Paul II to the religious of Brazil, July 11, 1986, n. 5; cf. Introduction, note 5.

40. *Lumen Gentium*, n. 44.

41. *Renovationis Causam*, n. 5; cf. Introduction, note 7, above.

42. "Final Document of the Special Synod of Bishops of the Low Countries," *L'Osservatore Romano*, Feb. 2, 1980, proposition 32.

43. John Paul II, apostolic letter *Mulieris Dignitatis* (1988), n. 7.

44. *Ibid.*, n. 6.

45. *Ibid.*, n. 7.

46. John Paul II, Apostolic Exhortation *Christifidelis Laici* (1989), n. 50.

47. *Ibid.*

48. *Ibid.*, encyclical *Redemptoris Mater* (1987), n. 46.

Chapter 3

1. Cf. *Renovationis Causam*, n. 4; Introduction, note 7, above.

2. Cf. Canon 597.2.

3. Cf. Canon 641-645.

4. See above nn. 26-30.

5. Cf. Canon 620.

6. Canon 646.

7. *Lumen Gentium*, n. 44.

8. *Ibid.*, n. 46.

9. Canon 652.1.

10. Canon 648.2.

11. *Renovationis Causam*, n. 5; cf. Introduction, note 7, above.

12. Canon 652.5.

13. Canon 650.1.

14. Cf. Canons 597.1-2, 641-645.

15. Cf. Canons 134.1, 1047.4.

16. Cf. Canons 647-649, 653.2.

17. *Lumen Gentium*, n. 46.b.

18. Cf. Canons 650-652.1.

19. Cf. Canon 985.

20. Canon 652.3.

21. Canon 652.4.

22. Cf. *Lumen Gentium*, n. 45.

23. Dated Feb. 2, 1970, a corrected re-edition was published in 1975.

24. John Paul II in Madrid, Nov. 2, 1982.

25. *Renovationis Causam*, n. 7; cf. Introduction, note 7, above.

26. Order of Religious Profession, n. 5; cf. note 24.

27. *Ibid.*, n. 6.

28. *Ibid.*

29. Cf. Canons 655-658.

30. Canon 659.1-2.

31. Canon 660.1-2.

32. Cf. Mk 8:31-37; 9:31-32; 10:32-34.

33. *Unitatis Redintegratio*, n. 11.

34. *Ratio Institutionis*, nn. 70-81 and note 148; n. 90-93.

35. *Mutual Relations,* n. 13a; cf. Introduction, note 8, above.

36. *Essential Elements,* II, n. 47; cf. Introduction, note 10, above.

37. *The Contemplative Dimension,* II, n. 11; cf. Introduction, note 9, above.

38. *Perfectae Caritatis,* n. 14; see also Canon 630.

39. *The Contemplative Dimension,* II, n. 11, cf. Introduction, note 9.

40. Cf. Canon 660.1.

41. *Mutual Relations,* n. 26; cf. Introduction, note 8.

42. Canon 661.

43. John Paul II to the religious of Brazil, 1986, n. 6; cf. Introduction, note 5, above.

44. *Mutual Relations,* nn. 11b, 12b, 23f; cf. Introduction, note 8.

45. Cf. *Perfectae Caritatis,* n. 2d.

46. 2 Cor 4:16; see also 5:1-10.

47. Jn 21:15-19.

48. Phil 3:10; cf. 1:20-26 and *Lumen Gentium,* n. 48.

Chapter 4

1. *Perfectae Caritatis,* n. 7.

2. *The Contemplative Dimension,* n. 26-27; cf. Introduction, note 9, above.

3. Heb 11:1.

4. *Ibid.,* 11:2.

5. Cf. *ibid.,* 11:27.

6. 1 Cor 13:12.

7. Origen, *Peri Archon,* 1.8.1.

8. Cf. *Lumen Gentium,* nn. 49, 50; *Sacrosanctum Concilium,* nn. 5, 8, 9, 10.

9. Paul VI to the major superiors of Italy (1966). See also his "Letter to the Carthusians," April 18, 1971.

10. *Presbyterorum Ordinis,* n. 13; cf. Paul VI, Encyclical *Mysterium Fidei.*

11. *Summa Theologica,* IIIa, Q. 82, a. 10.

12. *Ibid.,* IIa, IIae, Q. 189, a. 8, ad 2um.

13. *Lumen Gentium,* n. 46.

14. Instruction *Venite Seorsum,* III, Introduction and note 27.

15. St. Thérèse of the Child Jesus, *Autobiography,* 1957, p. 229.

16. Cf. Canon 667.

Chapter 5

1. *Gravissimum Educationis,* n. 2.

2. *Christifidelis Laici,* n. 46; cf. propositions 51-52 of the 1987 Synod of Bishops.

3. *Christifideles Laici*, n. 46.

4. International Theological Commission, Oct. 8, 1985, n. 4.I.

5. John Paul II to UNESCO, 1980, nn. 6-7.

6. *Lumen Gentium*, n. 46.

7. International Theological Commission, "Faith and Inculturation," nn. 8-22, cf. La Civita Cattolica 140.1 (1989) 159-177.

8. *Ibid.*, see also *Christifideles Laici*, n. 44.

9. International Theological Commission, nn. 4-2; see note 4 of this chapter.

10. *Christifideles Laici*, n. 55.

11. *Ibid.*, n. 30.

12. Cf. Canon 578.

13. Cf. *Christus Dominus*, n. 35.3-4; *Mutual Relations*, n. 13c.

14. Canon 586.

15. Canon 659.2; see also 650.1 for what concerns the novitiate in particular.

16. *Mutual Relations*, n. 13a; cf. Introduction, note 8, above.

17. *Lumen Gentium*, n. 25.

18. *Mutual Relations*, n. 33; cf. Introduction, note 8, above, and also Canons 753 and 212.1.

19. *Mutual Relations*, n. 28; cf. Introduction, note 8. For the "perfecter" bishops, see *Summa Theologica*, IIa-IIae, Q. 184.

20. Canons 650.1 and 659.2. See also John Paul II to the religious of Brazil, July 2, 1986, n. 5. Cf. Introduction, note 5, above.

Chapter 6

1. Canon 659.3.

2. First ed., Jan. 6, 1970; second ed., March 19, 1985.

3. Cf. Canons 242-256.

4. See *Optatam Totius*, nn. 2, 19-21; *Ad Gentes*, nn. 25-26.

5. Cf. Canons 1010-1054.

6. John Paul II to the religious of Brazil on July 10, 1980; cf. Introduction, note 5, above.

7. *Ibid.*

8. Cf. *Lumen Gentium*, n. 44.

9. Cf. *Perfectae Caritatis*, n. 8.

10. *Christus Dominus*, n. 35.2.

11. *Mutual Relations*, n. 23d.

12. *Ibid.*, n. 37.

13. *Christus Dominus*, n. 34. According to n. 35, *"ut episcopis auxiliatores adsint et subsint."*

14. *Mutual Relations*, n. 18b.

15. Cf. Canon 586.1-2.

16. Cf. Canon 591 and *Mutual Relations*, n. 23.
17. *Mutual Relations*, nn. 57-58; cf. Canon 520.2.

Conclusion

1. *Mutual Relations*, n. 6; Introduction, note 8, above.
2. *Redemptoris Mater*, n. 2.
3. *Ibid.*, n. 4.
4. *Ibid.*
5. *Lumen Gentium*, n. 42.

St. Paul Book & Media Centers

ALASKA
750 West 5th Ave., Anchorage, AK 99501; 907-272-8183

CALIFORNIA
3908 Sepulveda Blvd., Culver City, CA 90230; 310-397-8676
5945 Balboa Ave., San Diego, CA 92111; 619-565-9181
46 Geary Street, San Francisco, CA 94108; 415-781-5180

FLORIDA
145 S.W. 107th Ave., Miami, FL 33174; 305-559-6715

HAWAII
1143 Bishop Street, Honolulu, HI 96813; 808-521-2731

ILLINOIS
172 North Michigan Ave., Chicago, IL 60601; 312-346-4228

LOUISIANA
4403 Veterans Memorial Blvd., Metairie, LA 70006; 504-887-7631

MASSACHUSETTS
50 St. Paul's Ave., Jamaica Plain, Boston, MA 02130; 617-522-8911
Rte. 1, 885 Providence Hwy., Dedham, MA 02026; 617-326-5385

MISSOURI
9804 Watson Rd., St. Louis, MO 63126; 314-965-3512

NEW JERSEY
561 U.S. Route 1, Wick Plaza, Edison, NJ 08817; 908-572-1200

NEW YORK
150 East 52nd Street, New York, NY 10022; 212-754-1110
78 Fort Place, Staten Island, NY 10301; 718-447-5071

OHIO
2105 Ontario Street, Cleveland, OH 44115; 216-621-9427

PENNSYLVANIA
214 W. DeKalb Pike, King of Prussia, PA 19406; 610-337-1882

SOUTH CAROLINA
243 King Street, Charleston, SC 29401; 803-577-0175

TENNESSEE
4811 Poplar Ave., Memphis, TN 38117; 901-761-0874

TEXAS
114 Main Plaza, San Antonio, TX 78205; 210-224-8101

VIRGINIA
1025 King Street, Alexandria, VA 22314; 703-549-3806

GUAM
285 Farenholt Avenue, Suite 308, Tamuning, Guam 96911; 671-646-7745

CANADA
3022 Dufferin Street, Toronto, Ontario, Canada M6B 3T5; 416-781-9131